T0196570

God's Single Sisters
Newsletters

GLORIA BESS

WESTBOW
PRESS®
A DIVISION OF THOMAS NELSON
& ZONDERVAN

Copyright © 2018 Gloria Bess.

All rights reserved. No part of this book may be used or reproduced by any means, graphic, electronic, or mechanical, including photocopying, recording, taping or by any information storage retrieval system without the written permission of the author except in the case of brief quotations embodied in critical articles and reviews.

Scripture quotations are taken from the Holy Bible, New International Version®, NIV®. Copyright © 1973, 1978, 1984, 2011 by Biblica, Inc.™ Used by permission of Zondervan. All rights reserved worldwide.

This book is a work of non-fiction. Unless otherwise noted, the author and the publisher make no explicit guarantees as to the accuracy of the information contained in this book and in some cases, names of people and places have been altered to protect their privacy.

WestBow Press books may be ordered through booksellers or by contacting:

WestBow Press
A Division of Thomas Nelson & Zondervan
1663 Liberty Drive
Bloomington, IN 47403
www.westbowpress.com
1 (866) 928-1240

Because of the dynamic nature of the Internet, any web addresses or links contained in this book may have changed since publication and may no longer be valid. The views expressed in this work are solely those of the author and do not necessarily reflect the views of the publisher, and the publisher hereby disclaims any responsibility for them.

Any people depicted in stock imagery provided by Thinkstock are models, and such images are being used for illustrative purposes only.
Certain stock imagery © Thinkstock.

ISBN: 978-1-5127-6174-0 (sc)
ISBN: 978-1-5127-6173-3 (e)

Print information available on the last page.

WestBow Press rev. date: 05/21/2018

Table of Contents

Keeping the candles burning

Introduction…

As God's children we are here to encourage, support and lift up one another. And we urge our brothers and sisters, warn those who are idle encourage the timed, help the weak, be patient with everyone. Make sure that nobody pays wrong for wrong but always try to be kind to each other and to everyone else. Be joyful always' pray continually, give thanks in all circumstances for this is God's will for you in Christ Jesus ~ 1 Thessalonian. 4:14-18

Ladies let's keep our candles burning within our souls and our hearts. Her candle goesth not out by night ~ Proverbs 31:18

Peace and Blessings ~ Gloria Bess

Dedication...

*To the God of the most high and to the Holy Spirit I thank you for ministering
to me while I write and travel this journey.*

*To all Single Sisters I pray that God teach and touch you in a might way.
To all Mothers that are raising their children without a Father. I pray that God
strengthens you while you are raising your children and give you the patience and endurance to
be the Head of your household.*

*To my Mother (Doris) thank you for raising me to be a strong woman.
As a single mother without you I would not be able to endure the journey of Single
Motherhood.*

*To my children and grandchildren - Shanice (daughter), Jeremiah (son),
Neveah (granddaughter) and little Devon (grandson) I love you very much.
To my sisters and brothers Stephanie, Cherrice, Edgar and Roland thank you. I am
very blessed to have each one of you in my life.*

July – December

Peace …. Promise … Prosperity

Thanksgiving…Triumph…Truth

Newsletter I
July – December

Ransom – "Who gave himself a ransom for all, to be testified in due time" 1 Timothy 2:6

God's Single Sisters Newsletter

Verses and Scriptures Volume 1

Peace—inner contentment, calm, serenity, free from strife, to be silent

Genesis 41:16
Roman 3:17, 5:1, 10:15
Numbers 6:26,
Jeremiah 6:14, 8:15, 25:12 14:19, 34:5,
Deuteronomy 20:10, 23:6
Ezekiel 7:25,
1 Samuel 25:6
Matthew 10:13
Luke 10:5, 1:79
2 Kings 9:19
Job 5:23, 22::21

Quiet Time
O' that my life may be useful be as I serve Jesus faithfully, and may the world see Christ in me, this is my earnest prayer. The measure of your usefulness is the measure of your faithfulness.

The Son can do nothing of Himself - John 4:19

Solomon Says 🕊

An evil man is trapped by his sinful talk, but a righteous man escapes trouble. Proverbs 12:1

All about You....
Name five things that you did for someone that's honorable.

1.

2.

3.

4.

5.

In Christ Jesus Name

Verses and Scriptures

Contentment

Write your blessed name, O Lord upon my heart there to remain so indelibly engraved that no prosperity, nor adversity shall remove me from your love—Benjamin Harlin

When we invite the Lord to place his work of ownership on our lives, we acknowledge His wise and loving provision for all our needs— David McCasland

Contentment is realized that God has already given me all I need.
Give me neither poverty nor riches feed me with the food allotted to me. Proverbs 30:8

Peace

Look, there on the mountains the feet of one who brings good news, who proclaims peace! Nahum 1:15

Grace and peace be yours in abundance. 1 Peter 1:2

Translation of the Bible

I was asked one day how did I know that the Bible and its contents (scriptures and verses) were consistent to the original writings of the King James Version? The age-old questions throughout the centuries has been, was the bible rewritten incorrectly? Is it true that some scriptures that we read today has been tampered with, adding to or taking away for our own purposes? The Bible said: ***I warn everyone who hears the words of the prophecy of this book. If anyone adds anything to them, God will add to him the plagues described in this book and if anyone takes words away from this book of prophecy, God will take away from him his share in the tree of life and in the holy city, which are described in this book. Revelations 22:18-19.*** I truly believe that the book of 66 is so marvelous and divinely written from God mouth to the minds of scholars throughout the centuries. But don't take my word for it. Pray, study and read.

God's Favor

For his anger endured but a moment; in his favor endure for a night but joy, cometh in the morning—Psalm. 30:5

For thou, Lord, wilt bless the righteous; with favor wilt thou compass him as with a shield— Psalm. 5:12

Poem for the Month

<u>Living the Way We Pray</u>

I knelt to pray when day was done and prayed: "O Lord, bless everyone: Lift from each heart the pain, and let, the sick be well again." And then I woke one day, and carelessly went on my way, the whole day long I did not try to wipe a tear from any eye. I did not try to share the load of any brother on the road; I did not even go to see the sick man just next door to me. Yet once again when day was done I prayed: "O Lord, bless everyone." But as I prayed, to my ear there came a voice that whispered clear: "Pause, hypocrite, before you pray: Whom have you tried to bless today? God's sweetest blessings always go by hand that serve him here below" and then I hid my face and cried: "Forgive me God for I have lied, let me but live another day, and I will live the way I pray." - Author Unknown

Seal It with a Prayer

Lord thank you for blessing me to have a roof over my head, food on the table, furniture in the house and breath in my body, Father I am content. Lord I thank you for this very first newsletter. I pray that as I go through this Journey that this ministry will grow and that the mustard seeds (words) in these newsletters will harvest and grow. In Christ Jesus Name Amen.

Name it and Claim It...

Pray this month that God teaches you to be content with what you have until He blesses you with more. Claim it, believe it and trust God for it. Stand still and watch God do it.

Author's Reflection

<u>*Peace*</u>

Peace is a daily, a weekly, a monthly process, gradually changing opinions, slowly eroding old barriers, quietly building new structures." ~ John F. Kennedy

"Be anxious for nothing, but in everything by prayer and supplication, with thanksgiving, let your requests be made known to God; and the peace of God, which surpasses all understanding, will guard your hearts and minds through Christ Jesus." -Philippians 4:6-7

God's Single Sisters Newsletter

Verses and Scriptures Volume 2

Promise– guarantee, give surety, pledge, swear, declare, reassure, comfort.

Number 14:40
Deuteronomy 1:11, 9:28, 19:8, 27:3
2 Kings 8:19
Mark 14:11

And this is the promise that He has promised us—eternal life. - 1 John 2:25

Perseverance
I'm pressing on the upward way, new heights I'm gaining every day, still praying as I'm onward bound, "Lord, plant my feet on higher ground." – Oatman

God loves us too much to let us stay as we are.

Solomon Says
A good name is more desirable than great riches to be esteemed is better than silver or gold. - Proverb 2:21

All about You....
Name five things that you promise you would do for yourself...

1.
2.
3.
4.
5.
In Christ Jesus Name

Verses and Scriptures
God's Care
Because God cares about us we can leave our cares with Him. God heals the brokenhearted and binds up their wounds. He counts the number of the stars; He calls them all by name. - Psalms 147:3-4

God's Strength
Under His wings I am safely abiding, though the night deepens and tempests are wild; still I can trust Him; I know He will keep me, He has redeemed me, and I am His child – Cushing

Poem for the Month

It Is Well With My Soul
When peace, like a river, attends my way. When sorrows like sea billows roll; Whatever my lot, Thou hast taught me to say, It is well, it is well with my soul. – Author Unknown

God of All Comfort
We understand that although suffering is not eradicated, we have someone who soothes us in the midst of it. Often we cry for even temporary pain relief, but the God of all comfort gives permanent consolation in the midst of excruciating pain.

Comfort is found not in the absence of pain but in the midst of it. So many hurting Christians believe their walk with Lord is not as it should be because of their intense pain. They don't feel comfortable. Feeling comfortable and being comforted are two different things. The first is a nice feeling but tends to come and go, as feelings do. The second is a fact based on the Comforter, not on circumstances.

And he does not come and go: "I will never leave you nor forsake you" -Hebrews 13:5

The Comforter soothes in various ways-through Scripture, through hymns, through other saints (who have probably been hurt), or through myriad tailor-made ways that suit the particular hurts. He is wonderfully creative, perfectly matching the comfort with the sorrow. "From Charles Stanley's book—The Glorious Journey"

My God It's Storming
Imagine being on a transit bus and just as soon as you get on the bus it starts to rain a little and then about mid-way of your journey it starts to thunder and lighten, now you're almost at your stop and it starts to pour and it's still thundering and lightening. You're thinking to yourself how am I going to get to the house, I got two blocks to walk and I left my umbrella on the job. The question is, if you were in this situation what would you do? Staying on the bus would not be good, the storm may last for hours or days you would've passed your stop over and over, nothing gain! Where is the victory! However, if you get off the bus and start to walk through the storm just like you would do if it wasn't storming, you will surely reach your destination and be out of the storm. Victory!

I said all of that to say this, don't sit around and let the storms get you depress, pick up and do what you normal do while it's storming with strength and perseverance and go on through that storm and reach your destination. In Christ Jesus Name Amen.

Seal It with a Prayer

Lord I thank you that your promises can not be broken. Lord I thank you for your promises of yesterday, today and tomorrow. In Christ Jesus Name Amen

Name it and Claim it...

Pray this month about the promises of God. Ask him to reveal his promises to you. Name it, claim it and trust God for it. Stand back and watch God do it.

Author's Reflection

Promise

Because of your promise, Lord, I can be still and calm even when it's hectic around me ~ Anon

I remember years ago, when I lived on Grantley Avenue I would visit the church down the street from my house, I really enjoyed the services, so I decided to visit the church again; I also noticed that they had a summer vacation bible camp for children, I wanted my daughter to go there for camp, so one day I went to inquire about the camp. I spoke with a church member who happens to be in charge of the camp. We began to talk, and I shared with her about the many storms that I had been through, and that I was still going through. We began to pray and after we finished praying, she said to me "God spoke into my spirit while we were talking and, he said he is going to bring you out of your wilderness. He's going to do some great things for you." Well at that time I was thirty-nine, so I was very excited to be turning forty. When I turned forty I look for the promise of coming out of the wilderness but instead I was going through more storms. It was at age forty-nine when I discovered that God was bringing me out of the wilderness by taking me through those storms. I am now fifty years old, and I am beginning to see things clearer than I did in my forties. I thank God for the storms and the wilderness.

In peace, I will lie down and sleep, for you alone, Lord, make me dwell in safety. ~ Psalm 4:8

God's Single Sisters Newsletter

Verses and Scriptures Volume 3

Prosperity— wealth, affluence, opulence, riches, success

1 Samuel 25:6
Job 15:21, 36:11
Psalm 30:6, 73:3, 35:27, 122:7
Proverbs 1:23
Ecclesiastes 7:14
Jeremiah 22:21
1 Kings 10:7

In this you greatly rejoice, though now for a little while, if need be, you have been grieved by various trials—1 Peter 1:6

Wisdom, Knowledge + Understanding= SUCCESS and the key to it is JESUS- G. Bess

Solomon Says 🕊
Reckless words pierce like sword, but the tongue of the wise bring healing truthful lips endure forever, but a lying tongue lasts only a moment—Proverbs 2:18-19

All about You....
Name five things that you are or would like to be successful in......
1.
2.
3.
4.
5.
In Christ Jesus Name

Verses and Scriptures
<u>Wisdom, Knowledge and Understanding</u>
In that night did God appear unto Solomon, and said unto him, ask what I shall give thee. And Solomon said unto God, Thou hast shewed great mercy unto David my father, and hast made me to reign in his stead. Now, O Lord God, let thy promise unto David my father be established: for thou has made me King over people like the dust of the earth in multitude. Give me now wisdom and knowledge that I may go and come in before this people: for who can judge this thy people that is so great? And God said to Solomon, because this was in thine heart, and thou hast not asked riches, wealth, or honor, nor the of thine enemies, neither yet hast asked long life; but hast asked wisdom and knowledge for thyself, that thou may judge people, over whom I have made thee king: Wisdom and knowledge is grated unto thee; and I will give thee riches, and wealth, and honor, such as none of the kings have had that have been before thee, neither shall there any after thee have the like. 1 Chronicles 2:7-12

Poem for the Month
<u>Success</u>
I've never known success to grow until it start with me and that success will never succeed until I set it free.

<u>I Felt For It........</u>
One day in July my daughter accepted a postal packet for me, she called me on the job to let me know that there had been a delivery, I asked her to open the package. Inside was a check, I ask her to open the check, the amount of the check was $3,480.00. I ask her to put the check away until I get home. Throughout the day I kept asking myself who, where, when and why would I received a check in that amount. When I arrived at my home I immediately looked at the check and receipt. I could not figure out why I received this amount of money, there were no explanation on the receipt only a name of the sender and address. I looked at the check it was drawn from the Bank of American in Texas, it was a cashier's check, and was water marked and the correct numbers were on the check. Still confused, I called the bank in Texas and the person on the other end said the check was legitimate and the funds was in the account. I began to shout and thank God, thinking to myself this is right on time. I went out to several places that evening to cash the check but no one could do it. So the next morning I went to a place where I normally cashed my pay checks. Being a regular customer, it was not a problems getting the check cashed. The next week when I went to purchase some stamps from the check cashing place one of the tellers told me that last check I cashed was counterfeit and that she would have to file a police report against me, even though she told the owner of the check cashing center that I had been a regular customer for quite a while. She also told him that this had never occurred before with other checks that was cashed by this customer. I was told that I would be prosecuted and put in jail. I started to cry because I could not believe this was happening to me.

However, because I was known there the teller spoke to the owner on my behalf again, and he agreed to do a contract with me stating that I would pay the center back biweekly until funds was paid back. My first payment was with the money I had left from the check. "Yawl" if I had gone to any other cash checking center where I was unknown I would have been put in jail and prosecuted. Be careful ladies of these Internet contests and unknown checks. Check things out. Satan try to slaughter me, but God put a ram in the bush that saved me. I rejoice because of that ram. So now I look at the whole experience as a Blessing from God when I needed it. In Christ Jesus Name, Amen. Have a Blessed and Prosperous Month.

Seal It with a Prayer

Lord I thank you for your faithfulness when things look lost you provide a way out of all situations. Jesus, thank you for the Ram in the Bush!!

Name It and Claim It

Pray that God gives you the blessing to succeed in the things that you are about to embark upon. Claim it, believe it and trust God for it. Stand still and watch God do it.

Author's Reflection

<u>*Success*</u>

Each successive moment in my existence is in your hands – Anon

I pray that everyone get this, because we have some people who are successful and don't know how to receive it and some successful "want to be(s)" do not know how to handle it and embrace what God has given them. SUCCESS IS NOTHING WITHOUT GOD?

The beatitude – Now when he saw the crowds, he went up on a mountain side and sat down. His disciples came to him, and he began to teach them saying:
Blessed are the poor in spirit for theirs is the kingdom of heaven.
Blessed are those who mourn, for they will be comforted.
Blessed are the meek, for they will inherit the earth.
Blessed are those who hunger and thirst for righteousness for they will be filled.
Blessed are the merciful, for they will be shown mercy.
Blessed are the pure in heart, for they will see God.
Blessed are the peacemakers for they will be called sons of God.
Blessed are those who are persecuted because of righteousness for theirs is the kingdom of heaven.
Blessed are you when people insult you, persecute you and falsely say all kinds of evil against you because of me.
Rejoice and be glad, because great is your reward in heaven, for in the same way they persecuted the prophets who were before you. – Matthew 5:1-12

Rejoice and allow God to bless your success.

Do not boast about tomorrow, for you do not know what a day may bring – Proverbs 27:1

God's Single Sisters Newsletter

Verses and Scriptures Volume 4

Thanksgiving   <u>Thanks</u>— gratitude, appreciation, recognition, credit, merit

<u>Giving</u>—charitable, generous, openhanded philanthropic, benevolent

<u>Thanks</u>	<u>giving</u>
Nehemiah 12:31	Genesis 28:22
Matthew 26:27	Exodus 30:15
Luke 2:38	Deuteronomy 15:10, 16:17
Ephesian. 5:20	Ezekiel 46.5
1 Thessalonians 3:9 1	1 Chronicles 29:14
Revelations 4:9	Ezra 9:9
	Psalms 2:8, 6:5, 29:11,37:4-21, 84:11, 109:4,
	Isaiah 55:10

How precious is your loving kindness, O'God—Psalms 36:7

<u>Charity</u>

We all forget that one time or another someone had to give us a penny to make a nickel because we only had four cents. Or a neighbor who gave our mother flour to fry chicken or sugar to make "kool-aide" when we did not have it. Think on these things during the Holidays and beyond, *be charitable to someone Who Just Don't Have It.*

Verses and Scriptures

<u>Gratitude</u>

Consider what the Lord has done through those who've shown you love; then: thank them for their faithful deeds for blessing from above. Gratitude should not be an occasional incident but a continuous attitude!

I commend to you Phoebe for indeed she has been a helper of many and of myself. Roman 16:1-2

The Psalmist Says 🎵

Shout for joy to the Lord all the earth Worship the Lord with gladness; come before him with joyful songs now the Lord is God. It is he who made us, and we are his, we are his people and the sheep of his pasture.— 100:1-3

All about You....
Name five things that you're Thankful for...

1.

2.

3.

4.

5.

In Christ Jesus Name

Interesting Facts
 Did you know that...
- *Noah was the first person in the Bible to get drunk.*
- *Bethel meant "house of God" Jacob name it because God spoke to him there. Bethel became an important city and place. A place where the Israelites worshiped God.*
- *Sodom and Gomorrah ruins most likely lie under water at the south end of the Dead Sea.*
- *It is said that today the nation of Israel has oil wells near where Sodom and Gomorrah once stood*
- *The tabernacle was a tent church where the Israelites worshiped God*
- *In the book of Numbers the tabernacle was in the center of the camp. It was called the Tent of Meetings that is where God met with his people. Each Israelite tribe had its own area to the north, south, east or west of the tabernacle*
- *Ashdod and Ekron were Philistine cities. The Philistines had five large cities these two were the most powerful of the five.*

Give
Each one must give as he has decided in his heart, not reluctantly or under compulsion, for God loves a cheerful giver. - 2 Corinthians 9:7

Glory – give it all to God

Initiative – you have the power and opportunity to bless others

Valuable – be useful and helpful

Educate – knowledge is a powerful tool, teach someone

Thanksgiving
JUDGE me O' Lord for I have walked in mine integrity: I have trust also in the Lord; therefore I shall not slide. Examine me, O' Lord, and prove me; try my reins and my heart. For them Loving kindness is before mine eyes: and I have walked in thy truth. I have not sat with vain persons neither will I go in with dissemblers. I have hated the congregation of evil doers; and will not sit

with the wicked. I will wash my hands in innocence: so will I compass, thine altar, O' Lord: that I may publish with the voice of thanksgiving, and tell of all thy wondrous works. Lord I have loved the habitation of thy house, and place where thine honor dwells. Gather not my soul with sinners nor my life with bloody men: in whose hand is mischief and their right hand is full of bribes. But as for me, I will walk in mine integrity: redeem me, and be merciful unto me. My foot stand in an even place in the congregations will I bless the Lord. - Psalms 26

Seal It with a Prayer
Lord I thank you for this day of thanksgiving. I thank you every day for the blessings of the past, the blessings of the present and the blessings of the future. In Christ Jesus Name Amen.

Name It and Claim It...
Pray this month that Jesus teaches you to be giving to others and thankful for the things He has given you. Name it, claim it, believe it and trust God for it. Stand back and watch God do it.

Author's Reflection

Giving

The mystery is too great for me: Dying, you gave me life. Giving you gathered us all. So I simply accept. ~ Anon

Many women were there, watching from a distance. They had followed Jesus from Galilee to care for his needs. Among them were Mary Magdalene, Mary the mother of James and Joses, and the mother of Zebedee's sons. ~ Matthew 27:55-56

When the Sabbath was over, Mary Magdalene, Mary the mother of James and Salome bought spices so that they might go to anoint Jesus' body. ~ Mark 16:1

While they were wondering about this suddenly two men in clothes that gleamed like light stood, beside them. In their flight the women bowed down with their faces to the ground, but the men said to them Why do you look for the living among the dead? ~ Luke 24:4-5

They asked her, "Woman why are you crying? They have taken my Lord away," She said "and I don't know where they have put him." At this she turned around and saw Jesus standing there, but she did not realize that it was Jesus. "Woman," he said, "Why are you crying? Who is it you are looking for?" Thinking he was the gardener, she said, "Sir if you have carried him away, tell me where you have put him, and I will get him. Jesus said to her, "Mary" She turned toward him and cried out in Aramaic "Rabboni" (which means Teacher). ~ John 20:13-16
There is one God; there is also one mediator between God and humankind, Christ Jesus, himself human who gave himself as ransom for all ~ 1 Timothy 2:5-6

God's Single Sisters Newsletter

Verses and Scriptures Volume 5

Triumph- victory, achievement, success, conquest, accomplishment

Psalms 25:2, 47:7, 92:4
2 Corinthians 2:14
Colossians 2:15
2 Samuel 1:20
Job 20:5

Victory
From the womb to the cradle, from the cradle to his ministry, from the ministry to the cross from the cross to the grave from the grave to the sky.

VICTORY.......

Have a Blessed Day—G. Bess

Verses and Scriptures
Thankful for Seasons
Just as the winter turns to spring, our lives have changing seasons too; so when a gloomy forecast comes. Remember- God has plans for you.—Sper

To everything there is a season, a time for every purpose under heaven—Ecclesiastes 3:1

The Psalmist Says 🎵
In you, O' Lord I have taken refuge; let me never be put to shame; deliver me in your righteousness. Turn your ear to me come quickly to my rescue; be my rock of refuge a strong fortress to save me. —31:1-2

All about You....
Name five things that have been victorious in your life...
1.
2.
3.

4.

5.

In Christ Jesus Name

<u>Interesting Facts</u>

Did you know that...

- *In the book of Esther providence means a word used to talk about God's control of everything that happens.*
- *In the book of Matthews the beatitudes are a special saying of Jesus, explaining how to be blessed or truly happy.*
- *Women in biblical times used clay ovens to bake their bread. They would build a fire inside and when the oven was hot they would put a pan cake shape bread on the outside to cook.*
- *A parable is a special kind of story. It teaches a lesson by saying what something is like*
- *Missionaries are people who travel to tell others about Jesus the first two missionary of the Christian church were Barnabas and Paul (Saul).*
- Synagogues is where Jews gathered each Sabbath to worship. *At the front of the* synagogues was a container called an ark where the Bible scrolls was kept.

<u>Achievements</u>

I can do all things through Christ who strengthens me. - Philippians 4:13

Acquire – learn a skill, develop good habits

Character – be personable, pleasant and amiable it means a lot

Humble – having a respectful and submissive spirit goes a long way

Impressive – first impression is a lasting impression

Even Tempered – keep your temper at an even level be pleasant and calm

Vanquish – become a victorious woman

Earn - celebrate your achievements, you earned it!

<u>The Reason for the Season</u>

And there were in the same country shepherds abiding in the field, keeping watch over their flock by night. And, lo, the Angel of the Lord came upon them, and the glory to the Lord shone round about them: and they were sore afraid. And the angel said unto them, Fear not: for behold, I bring you good tidings of great joy, which shall be to all people. For unto you is born this day in the city of David a Savior, which is Christ the Lord and this shall be a sign unto you: Ye shall find the babe wrapped in swaddling clothes, lying in the manger. And suddenly there was with the angel a multitude of the heavenly host praising God, and saying, Glory to God in the highest, and on earth peace, good will toward men, and it came to pass, as the angels were gone away from them into heaven, the shepherds said one to another, Let us now go even unto Bethlehem, and see this thing which is come to pass, which the Lord hath made known unto us, and they came with haste, and found Mary and Joseph, and the babe lying in a manger, and when they had seen it, they made known abroad them saying which was told them concerning this child, and all they that heard it wondered at those things which were told them by the Shepherds. But Mary kept all these things, and pondered them in her heart. And the shepherds returned, glorifying and praising God for all the things that they had heard and seen, as it was told unto them. And when eight days were accomplished for the circumcising of the child, his name was called JESUS, which was so named of the angel before he was conceived in the womb. Luke 2:8-21

Seal It with a Prayer
Lord kept reminding me that I must celebrate your birth each day throughout the year, to keep me abreast of the things that you are birthing in me.—In Christ Jesus Name Amen

Be Careful...
*During the holiday season and every day we need to take precautions and be aware of our surroundings, we want to be able to celebrate the holiday's un-harm, be carefully when you go shopping, **ALWAYS** be in groups of two or more or whenever possible take a male. Have A Blessed and Safe Holiday.—G. Bess.*

Name it and Claim it...
Pray this month that God gives you Joy and Peace for the Holiday season. Claim it, believe it and trust God for it. Stand still and watch God do it.

Author's Reflection

Triumph

Ministers of the New Covenant ~ Not when I went to Troas to preach the gospel of Christ and found that the Lord had opened a door for me, I still had no peace of mind, because I did not find my brother Titus there. So I said good bye to them and went on to Macedonia.

But thanks be to God, who always leads us in triumphal procession in Christ and through us in spreads everywhere the fragrance of the knowledge of him. For we are to God the aroma of Christ among those who are being saved and those who are perishing. To the one we are the smell of death; to others the fragrance of life. And who is equal to such task? Unlike so many, we do not peddle the word of God for profit. On the contrary, in Christ we speak before God with sincerity, like men sent from God ~ 2 Corinthians 2:12-16

God's Single Sisters Newsletter

Verses and Scriptures Volume 6

Truth—fact, realty, honesty

John 4:19-26, 7:13-19, 8:31-41, 14:5-14
2 Timothy 2:8-26
2 John
3 John

There is a treasure you can own that's greater than a crown or throne: a conscience good with which to live that only God Himself can give.—Sendour

Conscience is like a sundial when the truth of God shines on it, it points in the right directions.

<u>Realty</u>
For God so loved the world that he gave his only begotten Son, That whosoever believeth in him should not perish but have everlasting life. For God sent not his Son unto the world to condemn the world; but that the world through him might be saved—John 3:16-17

Verses and Scriptures
<u>Honesty</u>
Lord who may dwell in your sanctuary? Who may live on your holy hill? He whose walks in the blameless and who does what be righteous, who speaks the truth from his heart and has no slander on his tongue, who does his neighbor no wrong and cost no slurs on his fellowman, who despise a vile man but honor those who fear the Lord, who keep his oath even when it hurts. Who lends his money without usury and does not accept a bribe against the innocent. He who does these things will never be shaken. – Psalms 15

Solomon Says 🕊
Better a little with righteousness than much gain with injustice. In his heart a man plans his course but the Lord determines his steps.—Proverbs 16:8-9

All about You....
Name five things that you have always been truthful about....

1.

2.

3.

4.

5.

In Christ Jesus Name

Interesting Facts
Did you know that...

- *In the biblical times clothes washing was simply dipped in water and beat with sticks. Some launderers used ashes to treat clothes and then whitened it in the sun.*
- *After David become king of the entire nation of Israel, and he led his army to take the city of Jerusalem from the Jebusites, upon winning this city, David took up residence in the fortress and called it the City of David.*
- *The Levite Jonathan, Saul, David and Jesus were all born in Bethlehem.*

Truth
And you will know the truth, and the truth will set you free - John 8:32

*T*estify – in truth and in spirit

*R*eceive- the word of God

*U*nderstand – where your strength comes from

*T*ake – refuge in God

*H*onest – to yourself and others

Seal It with a Prayer
Lord I thank you for teaching me the difference between the truth and a lie. A lie can keep you in bondage. The truth will set you free. In Christ Jesus Name Amen.

Halloween
The word Halloween or Hallowe'en dates back to 1745 and is of Christian origin. It comes from a Scottish term all Hollows Eve.

A brief history....

A group of farmers in Ireland, the Celts, planned a town party to keep the evil spirits happy. It is said that the farmers wore animal skin and went around the village collecting food and building barn fires to keep the spirits away. There are other historians who generally agreed that Halloween take place in ancient Druids.

Druids were a priestly class or educators of the Celtic religion. They believe in ceremonies and practices similar to the Indian religion. The Celts and Druid believed their New Year began November 1st and that October 31st marks the end of the old year. As a result of their belief, the Celts taught that on New Year Eve (our Halloween), ghosts, evil spirits and witches roamed the earth. In order to honor the sun god (Belenus) and to frighten away evil spirits the Celtic built large barn fires to keep the spirits away.

Reasons why we should not celebrated Halloween....
1. Halloween, Hallowe'en or All Halloween was a three-day holiday observed for the dead.
2. Its Satan's special day.
3. Halloween is associated with ghost, witches and spirits that roamed the earth.
4. People long ago worshiped statues believing that the souls of the wicked people who had died returned to harm, frighten and trick the living on Halloween. To keep those spirits away and from hurting them, they would try to be nice to them by placing sweets and other types of treats out. We call this "Trick or Treat".
5. God is a God of life – Halloween is about death.
6. Witchcraft is detestable to the Lord.
7. Finally, Halloween is Evil.

All Saints' Day
All Saints' day is defined as a festival, celebrate on November 1st, originated by the Roman Catholic. It is a day that honors all Saints known and unknown.

All Saints' day is known as All Hallows Day of all Saints', Solemnity Saints' and Feast of all Saints. In the early days the Christians were accustomed to celebrating the anniversary of a martyr's (victim) death for Christ at the place of martyrdom. In the fourth century, neighboring dioceses began to interchange feasts, to transfer relics, to divide them and to join in a common feast.

Name it and Claim it...
Pray this month that you can accept the truth about yourself and receive it. Name it, claim it and trust God for it. Stand back and watch God do it.

Author's Reflection

Truth

If we are wise, we will make discovering the truth about ourselves the work a lifetime. We will find that it is worth the honest effort. –Anon

Remember Jesus Christ, raised from the dead, descended from David. This is my gospel, for which I am suffered even to them who are not being chained like a criminal. But God's word is not chained. Therefore, I endure everything for the sake of the elect that they too may obtain the salvation that is in Christ Jesus, with eternal glory. Here is a trustworthy saying:

If we died with him, We will also live with him,
If we endure, we will also regain with him.
If we disown him He will disown us.
If we are faithless, He will remain faithful, for he cannot disown himself

Keep reminding them these things. Warn them before God against quarreling about words it is of no value and only ruins those who listen. Do your best to present yourself to God as one approved a workman who no need to be ashamed and who does correctly handle the word, of truth. Avoid godless chatters, because those who indulge in it will become more and more ungodly. Their teaching will spread like gangrene among them are Hymeaeus and Philetus who have wandered away from the truth. They say that the resurrection has already taken faith of some. Nevertheless, God stated with this inscription "The Lord knows who are his" and, "Everyone who confesses the name of the Lord must turn away from wickedness," -2 Timothy 2:8-19

Search me, O'God, and know my heart; test me and know my thoughts ~ Psalm 139:23

Newsletter II
January – December

Redeem – Let the redeem of the Lord say so, whom he hath redeemed from the hand of the enemy - Psalm 107:2

The Virtuous Woman
The Series
January – March

God's Single Sisters
Newsletter

Verses and Scriptures - January Volume 7

The Virtuous Woman

Virtuous – good, righteous, worthy, honorable, moral, upright and honest

Good

Genesis 14:21, 24:10, 50:20

Nehemiah 5:19, 13:31

Job 2:10, 22:21

Psalms 4:6, 14:1, 53:1

Matthew 12:29

Mark 3:27

Luke 6:30, 16:1, 19:8

Acts 10:38

1 Corinthians 13:3

Hebrews 10:34

Worthy

I baptize with water, John replied, "but among you stands one you do not know. He is the one who comes after me, the straps of whose sandals I am not worthy to untie" – John 1:26

Righteous

I love your truth, O Lord, The word which you have given; its precepts shall my soul delight on earth as well as heaven.—Bosch

Happiness is ours when we delight in the Lord. His righteousness endures forever—Psalm 112:9

Solomon Says

A Good name is rather to be chosen than great riches, and loving favor rather than silver and gold. The rich and poor meet together: the Lord is the maker of them all —
Proverbs 22:1-2

All about You....
Name five good things that happen to you.

1.

2.

3.
4.
5.
In Christ Jesus Name

Women of the Bible

Eve means – Life, living

And Adam said, this now bone of my bones and flesh of my flesh: she shall be call Woman, because she was taken out of Man. Therefore, shall a man leave his father and his mother, and shall cleave unto his wife: and they shall be one flesh. And they were both naked, the man and his wife, and were not ashamed. Genesis 2:23-25

The woman said to the serpent, "We may eat fruit from the trees in the garden, but God did say, 'You must not eat fruit from the tree that is in the middle of the garden, and you must not touch it, or you will die.'"

"You will not certainly die," the serpent said to the woman. "For God knows that when you eat from it your eyes will be opened, and you will be like God, knowing good and evil."

When the woman saw that the fruit of the tree was good for food and pleasing to the eye, and also desirable for gaining wisdom, she took some and ate it. She also gave some to her husband, who was with her, and he ate it. Then the eyes of both of them were opened, and they realized they were naked; so they sewed fig leaves together and made coverings for themselves. Genesis 3:2-7

Have you ever notice that...Adam did not name Eve right away she was called woman or his wife – G. Bess

<u>Virtuous Woman</u>
Give her of the fruit of her hands; and let her own works praise her in the gates - Proverbs 31:31

*V*aluable - be useful and helpful to your family but also too your neighbors.

*I*ntentions – plan something have an aim or purpose

*R*ighteous – have good and moral social behaviors

*T*reat – people the way you would like to be treated

*U*nderstand – people's feelings and their situations

*O*pportunity – to encourage someone

*U*nique – take on a task that no one wants

*S*acrifice – don't be selfish give up some of your time or things that you want, to help someone

The Virtuous Woman

Who can find a virtuous woman? For her price is far above rubies. The heart of her husband doth safely trust in her. So that, he shall have no need of spoil. She will do him good and not evil all the days of her life. She seeks wool, and Flax, and work willing with her hands. She is like the merchants' ships; she brings her food from afar. She rises also while it is yet night, and giveth meat to her household and portion to her maidens. She considers a field, and buy it: with the fruit of her hands she plant a vineyard. She girded her loins with strength, and strengthen her arms. She perceives that her merchandise is good; her candle goes not out by night. She lay her hands to the spindle, and her hands hold the distaff. She stretches out her hands to the poor; yea, she reaches forth her hands to the needy. She is not afraid of the snow for her household; for all her household are clothed with scarlet. She makes herself covering of tapestry; her clothing is silk and purple. Her husband is known in the gates when he sits among the elders of the land. She makes fine linens, and sells it; and delivered clothing; and she shall rejoice in time to come. She open her mouth with wisdom; and in her tongue is the law of kindness. She looks well to the ways of her household, and eat not the bread of idleness. Her children arise up and call her blessed; her husband also, and he praise her virtuously, but thou excellent them all. Favor is deceitful, and beauty is vain but a woman that feared the LORD, she shall be praised. Give her of the fruits of her hands; and let her own works praise her in the gates. Proverbs 31:10-31

Seal It with A Prayer

Jesus I pray that you would teach me how to become a virtuous woman through these series. Allow me to see me for who I am and give me the wisdom, knowledge and understanding, changing the things I cannot see.

Name it and Claim It...

Pray about something good that you really need in your life this month, thanking God not just for some things but for everything, claim it, believe it and trust God for it. Stand back and watch God do it.

Author's Reflection

Good

Do not be afraid little flock for it is your Father's good pleasure to give you the kingdom – Luke 12:32

On this New Year night I would like to reflect on the goodness of God. It is good to see the 31st of December at midnight rollover to a new beginning a New Year, to see your entire family wake up in the morning, to call people you love on that New Day and say Happy New Year asking them what their plans are for the year, to put away all of your problems your yesterdays and tomorrows just for that one moment, to be able to speak, taste, feel, walk and breath. It's good to hear laughter, not sorrow, to see the bare trees and feel the cold brisk January morning, to look at the parades on T.V.

and marvel at the beautiful sight it holds, to walk to your kitchen, bathroom or bed. It's good to breath, to feel the Life in you. It's good…

I am no longer content to feel myself at odds with the truth of your goodness. In this moment, I celebrate your involvement in the unfolding drama of my life's adventure ~ Anon.

God's Single Sisters Newsletter

The Virtuous Woman

Virtuous- good, righteous, worthy, honorable, moral, upright and honest

<u>Honorable</u>
Isaiah 3:3, 9:15, 42:21
Luke 14:8
1 Corinthians 4:10, 12:23

<u>Trust</u>
Sometimes it's hard to trust the Lord when we don't understand but fight the urge to run from Him-reach out and take His hand—Sper

<u>Expectation</u>
Jesus arose and conquered death; he robbed it of its fear and power; and one day he'll return to earth, though we know not the day nor hour—D. De Haan

God...has begotten us again to a living hope through the resurrection of Jesus Christ from the dead. – 1 Peter 1:3

<u>Ladies this is the year of Expectation, Pray, Hope and Trust</u>

Solomon Says 🕊

My Son, forget not my law but let thine heart keep my commandments: For length of days, and long life and peace, shall they add to thee. Let not mercy and truth forsake thee: bind them about thy neck; write them upon the table of thine heart: - Proverbs 3:1-3

All about You....
Name five things that you've done for people that are honorable
1.
2.
3.

4.

5.

In Christ Jesus Name

Women of the Bible

Sarai mean— my princess

And Abram and Nabor took them wives: the name of Abram's wife was Sarai and the name of Nahor's wife, Milcah, the daughter of Haran the father of Iscah. But Sarai was barren; she had no child. - Genesis 11:29-30

Hagar mean - flight, or according to others stranger

And the angel of the Lord said unto her, I will multiply they seed exceedingly, that it shall not be numbered for multitude. And the angel of the Lord said unto her, Behold, thou art with child, and shalt bear a son, and shalt call his name Ishmael; because the Lord hath heard thy affliction. And he will be a wild man; his hand will be against every man, and every man's hand against him; and he shall dwell in the presence of all his brethren. – Genesis 15:10-12

Have you ever notice that......

Sarai was later name Sarah and that Hagar worked for Sarah

And God said unto Abraham, as for Sarai they wife, thou shalt not call her Sarai but Sarah shall her name be. – Genesis 17:15

And Sarai said unto Abram, Behold now, the Lord hath restrained me from bearing: I pray thee, go in unto my maid; it may be that I may obtain children by her. And Abram hearkened to the voice of Sarai. - Genesis 16:2

Poem for the Month

<u>Do the Right Thing</u>

Okay, so your life is not as you planned, we all have our pitfalls, we all need a hand. We all get the chance to grab the brass ring, sometimes we fall short, just do the right thing, You have all the reasons to stand up and fight, for what you believe in, what we all know is right. Are your children hurting do you see them suffering, their future is yours now, just do the right thing. No one said it's easy to find your way home, yet the road is much smoother, when you're not all alone. Just open your heart to what Jesus can bring, the first step's the hardest, when you do the right thing—Unknown

<u>Seven Virtuous Women of the Bible</u>

Virtuous biblically is the Hebrew word chayil which means strong.

Virtuous having or showing high moral standard.

Synonyms: righteous, good, pure, saintly angelic, moral, ethical, upright, upstanding, high-minded, principled, exemplary

Virtue behavior showing high moral standards
Synonyms: goodness, virtuousness, righteousness, morality, integrity, dignity, rectitude, honor decency, respectability, nobility, worthiness, purity.

1. *Sarah* – Virtuous (high-minded)
        Virtue (nobility)
    Her husband is well-known he sets among the leaders of the land – Proverbs 31:23

2. *Ruth* – Virtuous (good)
        Virtue (goodness)
    She is like the merchants' ships she brings her food from afar – Proverbs 31:14
    She looks well to the ways of her household and does not eat the bread of idleness – Proverbs 31:27

3. *Rachel*– Virtuous (pure)
        Virtue (purity)
    Who can find a capable wife? Her value far exceeds the finest jewels. – Proverbs 31:10
    Her husband has full confidence in her; as a result, he lacks nothing of value. - Proverbs 31:11

4. *Jochebed* (Moses mother) – Virtuous (principled)
            Virtue (morality)
    She seeks out wool and flax, working with eager hands – Proverbs 31:13

5. *Shelometh* (mother to a blasphemer son – Leviticus) Virtuous (decency)
                Virtue (upright)
    She looks discretely to the affairs of her household, she's never lazy – Proverbs 31:27

6. Deborah – Virtuous (exemplary)
            Virtue (rectitude)
    Strength and honor are her clothing, and she shall rejoice in the time to come – Proverbs 31:25
    She opens her mouth with wisdom and in her tongue is the law of kindness – Proverbs 31:26

7. Hannah (Samuel mother) - Virtuous (*righteous*)
                Virtue (*righteousness*)
    Her children arise up, and call her blessed, her husband also, and he praised her – Proverbs 31:28

Many daughters have done virtuously, but thou excel them all. Favor is deceitful, and beauty is vain: but a woman that feared the Lord, she shall be praised. Give her of the fruit of her hands; and let her own works praise her in the gates. Proverbs 31:29-31

Seal It with a Prayer

Lord teach me how to honor you. Teach me how to honor my mother and father. Lord even when I do not feel like it, give me the spirit to honor other as well. I thank you, Jesus in your name only Amen

Name it and Claim it...

Pray about expectation in your life this month and claim it, believe it and trust God for it. Stand back and watch Jesus Do it!

Author's Reflection

This is Love

The months leading up to Valentine's Day; take a minute each month to do an inexpensive thing for someone.

March – Be patient with your children.

April – Be kind to a stranger.

May – Do not be envious to someone who may have more than you. Be happy for them.

June – Boasting is ugly! You are no better than the next person. The talents God gave you he will also give others. Encourage someone.

July – Do not be arrogant to someone. You have to remember that when you started someone was patient with you.

August – Do not be rude to people. Help them; it doesn't take but a minute.

September – Start your day off with a smile. Don't start your day being irritable. It messes up your day and sometimes everybody else's day.

October – Don't be resentful of others but rejoice with them. The Blessing will come to you in due season.

November – If someone has done you wrong do not wish that wrong comes back to them but pray for them and forgive.

December – Rejoice for other but rejoice because it's in your heart to do so not because at that moment you're showing off. Be true.

January – Love yourself, bear it, believe it, hope for it and endure it and in due season God will bless it. –

February (Valentine Day) – Remember this….
Love is patient, love is kind, love is not envious or boastful or arrogant or rude. It does not insist on its own way, it is not irritable or resentful; it does not rejoice in wrong doings. It bears all things, believe all things, hopes all things, and endures all things – 1 Corinthians 13:4-7

God's Single Sisters

Newsletter

Verses and Scripture ~ March Volume 9

The Virtuous Woman

Virtuous-good, righteous, worthy, honorable, moral, upright and honest

Moral
Roman 6:12, 8:11
1 Corthinians 15:53-54

Decent
Let me give of myself, fear Lord, always ready to sacrifice, willing to share what I hold dear, never deterred by the price –Hess

Solomon Says

But the way of the wicked is like deep darkness; they do not know what makes them stumble. My son pay attention to what I say; listen closely to my words. Do not let them out of your sight keep them within your heart for are life to those who find them and health to a man's whole body – Proverbs 4:19-22

All about You....
Name five things about yourself that's decent.

1.

2.

3.

4.

5.

In Christ Jesus Name

Women of the Bible

Milcah mean—counsel
Milcah was Nabor's Wife (Nabor was Abraham brother) Milcah had three sons.

Reumah mean—exalted, raised up
Reumah was in Nabor's concubine, and she had four sons.

Rebekah mean—captivating
The wife of Isaac and the mother of Jacob and Esau.

Rachael mean—ewe, "the daughter"
Rachael is the sister to Leah and Jacob's second wife. She had two children and ten grandchildren.

Leah mean—weary
Leah is the sister to Rachael and first wife of Jacob. She had seven children, six boys and one girl. The daughter name was Dinah. Dinah mean – judge, vindicated. Leah had twenty-nine grandchildren

Bilhah means—faltering, bashful
Bilhah was Rachel's maidservant, and she had two children and five grandchildren by Jacob

Zilpah mean—drooping
Zilpah was Leah's maidservant, she had three sons and one daughter (the daughter name was Serah. Serah mean—abundance, princess. Serah had two sons and eleven grandchildren by Jacob.

Single Mothers
But I trust in your unfailing love; my heart rejoices in your salvation. I will sing the Lord's praise, for he has been good to me. – Psalms 13:5-6

Sacrifice – no sacrifice is greater for her children

Immediate – there's no delay response when it comes to her children

Natural – it's natural for her to make mistakes because this is how she learns to rise her children

Generous – her spirit is genuine, unconditional and gentle

Love – no one can doubt her love for her family

Excellent - she works very hard and is good at what she does

Women
Now Laban (who was Rebekah's brother) had two daughters' the name of the oldest was Leah and the name of the younger was Rachel. Leah had weak eyes but Rachel was lovely inform and beautiful.

Jacob was in love with Rachel and said "I'll work for you seven years in return for your younger daughter Rachel." Genesis 29:16-18. Then Jacob said to Laban, "Give me my wife, my time is completed and I want to lie with her". So Laban brought together all the people of the place and gave a feast. But when evening came, he took his daughter Leah and give her to Jacob and Jacob laid with her. When morning came, there was Leah? So Jacob said to Laban, "What is this you have done to me? I served you for Rachel, didn't I? Why have you deceived me?" Laban replied "It is not our custom here to give the younger daughter in marriage before the older one". Genesis 29:21-26.

Have you ever notice that......Rachel was jealous of Leah. When Rachel saw that she was not bearing Jacob any children she became jealous of her sister. So she said to Jacob "Give me children, or I'll die!" - Genesis 30:1

This jealousy tickled down to Jacob's children but in reverse. Leah's children was jealous of Rachael's children - Genesis 37:11

God's Woman

God is teaching me to be a true and good woman of virtue, where my emotional, physical, mental, moral and spiritual value will shine brighter than the most precious of gems. God is preparing me for my husband who will know that I will richly satisfy his needs. I will share all my wisdom and knowledge and understanding with him so that he may be adoptable to those things he does not understand. I will gather the healthiest of foods and ideas that are necessary to create good things with my hands. I will not be lazy in preparing his meals; I will support him in his dreams. I will take care of my household. I will consider and plan my career carefully before venturing into it and also I will plant my seeds into good soil. I am a hard worker and a very energetic woman who watches for bargains. I will help the poor, and generously help those in need, never turning away from those who ask for assistance. I will always pray and have no fear for what the future holds for my household, because God holds the future. My house and clothing will stay clean, my bed will be pure. My husband will sit in the present of his own business and I will be at his side. I will be creative in everything I do. When God sends my husband, God would have already taught me how to be strong and dignify, even at my age. When I speak, I will speak words of wisdom, I will know when to play and when to be serious, and my personality will be kind. Laziness will not be part of my makeup. I will hold my household together and pray for my children and husband continually. My children will call me blessed. My husband, will sit around his friends and praises me with these words "there are many good women, but my wife is the best of them all."

I know that charm can be deceptive, and outward beauty doesn't last, but a woman who fear and reverences God shall be greatly praised. She will be praised for the many wonderful things she does. Her good deeds shall bring her honor and recognition from God, and from those who are important in her life. Who can find a virtuous woman?

Here I am! (*Base on Proverbs 31:10-31*)

Seal It with a Prayer

Jesus teach me to be a good, true and a decent woman. Teach me how to handle things when I am upset. Teach me how to embrace, endure and humble myself in all things. In Christ Jesus Name Amen

Name it and Claim it...

Pray this month about things that is just and moral. Pray that these things will be a part of your life as a woman. Claim it, believe it and trust God for it. Stand back and watch Jesus Do It!

Author's Reflection

Morality

Ethics too, are nothing but reverence for life that is what gives me the fundamental principle of morality, namely, that good consist in maintaining, promoting and enhancing life, and that destroying, injuring, and limiting life are evil. ~ Anon

When I was a teen and well into my thirties I used to let words and actions get the best of me. I would wish bad things on people who hurt me. I would become very defensive when someone criticized me. I would argue the issue and keep it going for days. But now that I am older I learn to reverence life. I learn that good consist of maintaining my attitude. I look at things not as being a put down, but a put up. I've learned that being overlooked on the job, going through financial hardships, and raising my children without a father taught me and did not destroy me. There were no injuries in the process, but only preparations to promote me in due season.

Shun youthful passion and pursue righteousness, faith, love, and peace, along with those who call on the Lord from a pure heart. ~ 2 Timothy 2:22

Women of Excellence
The Series
April – September

God's Single Sisters
Newsletter

Verses and Scriptures - April Volume 10

Women of Excellency

Excellence—contempt, resourceful, trustworthy, confidence, wisdom, strength, beauty, fineness, distinction, quality, merit

Contempt
Roman 6:12, 8:11
Daniel 12:2
Esther 1:18
Job 31:34
Psalms 119:22

Wisdom
Not what we have, but what we use, not what we see, but what we choose, these are the things that damage or bless the sum of human happiness—Anon

How much better to get wisdom than gold! And to get understanding is to be chosen rather than silver—Proverbs 16:16

A little wisdom is better than a lot of wealth

Witness
Love divine, all loves excelling, Joy of heaven to earth comes down; fix in us Thy humble dwelling, all Thy faithful mercies crown—Wesley

Solomon Says
The Wisdom Woman builds her house, but with her own hands the foolish one tears her down. - Proverbs 14:1

All about You.......
Name five things about yourself that you are content with
1.
2.

3.
4.
5.
In Christ Jesus Name

Women of the Bible

Bashemath mean - sweet smelling
Wife of Esau (Jacob's bother)

Asenath mean – "gift of the sun-god" an Egyptian name
Joseph's wife

Shiphrah mean –beauty
One of the Egyptian midwives

Puah mean –splendid
One of the Egyptian midwives

And the king of Egypt spoke to the Hebrew midwives, of which the name of the one was Shiphrah, and the name of the other Puah: and he said When ye do the office of a midwife to the Hebrew women, and see them upon the stools; if it be a son, then ye kill him; but if it be a daughter then she shall live. - Exodus 1:16

But the midwives feared God, and did not as the king of Egypt commanded them, but saved the men children alive. - Exodus 1:17

Poem for the Month

Easter Is a Time of Love
Easter is a time of love, a time of death and pain undone, so we may know the power of the love that lives in everyone. Each love we feel, unstained and free, redeems us-as with you and me.—unknown

Happy Christmas—Happy Easter
Jesus our Savior left heaven above, coming to earth as a Servant with love; laying aside all His glory, He came, Bringing salvation through faith in His name. Christmas and Easter two chapters of the same Book. - Hess

Women of Excellence – Resourcefulness
Resource- *the ability and creativity to cope with difficulties*
Resourceful – *able to be skillful and prompt with new situations*

Deborah – was Israel's forth Judge of that time. She was a prophet.

She was resourceful by:
Being prompt in new situations

> She regularly took her seat under the Palm tree of Deborah between Ramah and Bethel in the mountain region – Judges 4:4-5

> She made decisions to Israelis who approached her in all situations.

Being creative with difficulties

> She sent for Barak from Kedesh-Naphtali. She asked him "The Lord God of Israel has command you, haven't he?" He told you Go out to Mount Tabor, and take 10,000 men with you from the tribes of Naphtali and Zebulun. I will draw out Sisera the commanding officer of Jabin's army, along with his chariots and troops, to the Kishon River, where I will drop him right into your hands – Judges 4:6-7

Having coping skills

> "If you go with me, I'll go", Barak replied, She responded "I will surely go with you, but the road that you're about to take will not lead to honor you." The Lord will sell Sisera into the hands of a woman. - Judges 4:8

Being resourceful
1. Research your resources
2. Be prompt in all situations
3. Be creative
4. Don't let difficult situations get in your way

Enemies that rob you of your resources
1. Procrastination
2. Disorganization
3. Unrealistic expectations

Seal It with a Prayer
Lord there are many things that you have given us and wisdom is one. Lord continues to keep me wise over things that are handed over to me. Continue to teach me how to think before I act. In Christ Jesus Name Amen.

Name it and Claim it...

Pray this month that you are quick to pass on resources that was given to you when you needed it. Don't hold on to it Pass it on.... Claim it, believe it and trust God for it. Stand back and watch Jesus Do It!

Author's Reflection

<u>*God's Relationship to Wisdom*</u>

The Lord brought me forth as the first of his works before his deeds of old I was appointed from eternity from the beginning, before the world began.

When there were no oceans, I was given birth, when there were no springs abounding with water; before the mountains were settled in place, before the hills was given birth, before he made the earth or its fields or any of the dust of the world.

I was there when he set the heavens in place, when he marked out the horizon on the face of the deep, when he established the cloud's above and fixed securely the fountains of the deep, when he gave the sea its boundary so the waters would not overstep his command and when he marked out the foundations of the earth. Then I was the craftsman at his side. I was filled with delight day after day, rejoicing always in his presence, rejoicing in his whole and delighting in mankind. ~ Proverbs 8:22-31

God's Single Sisters
Newsletter

Verses and Scriptures - May Volume 11

Women of Excellency

Excellence—contempt, resourceful, trustworthy, confidence, wisdom, strength, beauty, fineness, distinction, quality, merit

Trustworthy
Job 13:15, 39:11
Psalms 25:2, 31:6, 55:23, 143:8, 118:8, 144:2
Isaiah 50:10

Morning—His compassion fail not they are new every morning; great is Your Faithfulness—Lamentations—3:22-23

Noon—He makes me to lie down in green pastures; He leads me besides the still waters—Psalms 23:2

Evening—When He had sent the multitudes away, He went up on the mountain by Himself to pray. Now when evening come, He was alone there—Matthews 14:23

Mistaken Confidence
You can't earn your way into heaven—the wages from sinning is death. Jesus is longing to save you from sin; don't wait till you draw your last breath—Hess

You were not redeemed with corruptible things...but with the precious blood of Christ. - 1 Peter 1:18-19

Solomon Says 🕊
To man belong the plans of the heart, but from the Lord comes reply of the tongue. Honest scales and balances are from the Lord; all the weights in the bag are his making—Proverbs 16:1, 11

All about You.......
Name five things that makes you trustworthy
1.

2.

3.

4.

5.

In Christ Jesus Name

Women of the Bible

Rahab mean—wide, broad and large

Was a harlot who lodge and hid the two men Joshua sent in the city of Shittim in the Land of Jericho from the King. When the city of Jericho fell —Rahab and her family were preserved according to the promise of the spies, and were incorporated among the Jewish people. Joshua 6:17-25

Achsah mean –anklet

Caleb's only daughter. She was offered in marriage to the man who would lead an attack on the city of Debir or Kirjath-sepher. This was done by Othniel who accordingly obtain her as his wife. - Joshua 15:16-19; Judge 1:9-15

Deborah mean—a bee, spirited woman or women of fire

A judge and prophetess, the wife of Lapidoth, Jabin, the king of Hazor. Deborah roused the people from their lethargy. Her fame spread far and wide. She became a "mother in Israel". And "the children of Israel came up to her for judgments" as she sat in her tent under the palm tree "between Ramah and Bethel." - Judge 4:6, 14; 5:7

Poem for the Month

Influence of Godly Moms

Of all the earthly things God gives, there's one above all other: it is the precious, priceless gift of loving Christian mothers.—Anon

The virtues of mothers are visited on their children—Dickens

Women of Excellence – Trustworthiness

Trustworthy *– deserving of trust or confidence; dependable, reliable*

Trust *– Reliance on the integrity, strength, ability, surety of a person or thing confidence. Phoebe, Priscilla & Aquila*

Phoebe was a deaconess at the church in Cenchrea

They were trustworthy by:

Being accepted by the church

Welcome her in the Lord as is a appropriate for saints, and provide her with anything she may need from you, for she has ministered to many people, including me – Romans 16:1-2

Paul asked the church to welcome Phoebe because she was a trustworthy person who was a reliable and dependable saint. He asked the church to provide her with anything she may need, she has worked for the Lord and ministered to many people including Paul.

They were dependable and reliable by:

Having Paul's back

Greet Priscilla & Aquila, who work with me for the Messiah Jesus, and who risked their necks for my life. I am thankful to them, and so are all the churches among the gentiles - Romans 16:3-4

Wow! These three ladies were dependable, reliable and confident. To God Be the Glory!

Being Trustworthy is:

1. knowing what to do and say
2. being reliable
3. being confident
4. being honest
5. being loyal
6. being dependable

Enemies that rob you of your trustworthiness

1. complacency
2. manipulative
3. criticism
4. sharing

Seal It with a Prayer

Lord you send so many people across my feet to confide in me with their problems or their innermost secrets or feelings. Jesus remind me not to portray them, to keep it confidential, teach me to be trustworthy. In Christ Jesus Name Amen.

Name it and Claim it...

Pray this month about being trustworthy. Claim it, believe it and Hey, Trust God for it and stand back and watch Jesus do it.

Author's Reflection

Mothers

Today I recall the parents you gave me, who had such moments of goodness; for all that they are and were for me, may I harbor gratitude within me – and honor them for every attempt at love – Anon

Today I thought back to the age of 9 when my father pass, how afraid my mother must have been, she had 5 children ages ranging 1,2,7,9,12. She must have thought over and over how in the world! You see my father worked he was the bread and meat. My mother was a stay home mom she did not work. I can imagine how God most have, at that moment my father took his last breath, gave my mother the strength that she needed and my mother never knew. I also think back of how my mother must have cried herself to sleep many of nights without us knowing, how God must have given her comfort. My Mother must have grieved silently day after day but smiled when her children was around.

Then I look back at when I lost my daughter's father and the same thing happen to me and how I inherited my mother's strength and endurance. I thank God for mothers. I thank God for their strength, endurance, perseverance and love in all situations and in all circumstances. – In Jesus Name Amen.

Honor your Father and your Mother so that your days may be long in the land that the Lord our God is giving you – Exodus 20:12

God's Single Sisters Newsletter

Verses and Scriptures - June Volume 12

Women of Excellency

Excellence—*contempt, resourceful, trustworthy, confidence, wisdom, strength, beauty, fineness, distinction, quality, merit*

Confidence
Psalms 118:8
Proverbs 3:26
Ephesians 3:12
Philippians 3:3
Hebrews 3:6

Walking
I'd rather walk in the dark with God than go alone in the light; I'd rather walk by faith with him then go alone by sight.—Anon

We walk by faith, not by sight – 2 Corthinians 5:7

Give Thanks
Oh, render thanks to God above, the fountain of love, whose mercy firm through ages past has stood, and shall forever last.—Anon

It is good to give thanks to the Lord, and to sing praises to your name, O Most High – Psalms 92:1

The Psalmist Says 🎵
My Soul finds rest in God alone; he alone is my rock and my salvation; he is my fortress I will never be shaken.— 62:1

All about You.......
Name five things that you thank God for every day...
1.
2.
3.

4.

5.

In Christ Jesus Name

Women of the Bible

Delilah mean – languishing

Samson mistress who was bribed by the "lords of the Philistines" to obtain from Samson the secret of his strength and the means of overcoming it. She tried on three occasions to obtain from him this secret in vain. On the fourth occasion she wrung it from him. She made him sleep upon her knees, and then called the man who was waiting to help her; who "cut off the seven locks of his head," and so his "strength went from him." -Judges 16:4-18

Naomi mean- the lovable; my delight

The wife of Elimelech, and mother of Mahlon and Chilion, and mother-in-law of Ruth. Naomi longs to return now to her own land, to Bethlehem. One of her widowed daughters-in-law, Ruth, accompanies her, and is at length married to Boaz - Ruth 1:2, 20, 21; 2:1

Ruth mean -- a friend

A Moabitess, the wife of Mahlon. On the death of Elimelech and Mahlon, Naomi came with Ruth, her daughter-in-law, who refused to leave her, to Bethlehem, the old home from which Elimelech had migrated. There she had a rich relative, Boaz, to whom Ruth was eventually married. She became the mother of Obed, the grandfather of David.

Thus Ruth, a Gentile, is among the maternal progenitors of our Lord Matthew 1:5

Hannah mean- favor, grace

This was the name of one of the wives of Elkanah the Levite, and the mother of Samuel. -Samuel 1:2

Poem for the Month

Success

She has achieved success who has lived well, laughed often, and loved much; who has enjoyed the trust of pure women, the respect of intelligent men and the love of little children; who has filled her niche and who has left the world better than she found it whether by an improved poppy a perfect poem or a rescued soul; who has never lacked appreciation of earth's beauty or failed to express it; who has always looked for the best in others and given them the best she had; whose life was an inspiration; who memory a benediction.—Bessie Anderson Stanley (1904)

Women of Excellence – Confidence

Confidence– *belief in oneself and one's powers or abilities; self-confidence; self-reliance and assurance*

Manoah's wife (Samson's Mother)

She was self-assured:

The angel assured her that she would conceive and it would be a baby boy.

A certain man of Zorah, named Manoah, from the clan of the Danites, had a wife who was childless, unable to give birth. The angel of the Lord appeared to her and said, "You are barren and childless, but you are going to become pregnant and give birth to a son."– Judges 13:1-3

She believed in herself:

Then the woman went to tell her husband. She said "A man of God appeared to me. He looked like what an angel of God would look like, very frightening." I didn't ask him where he had come from, and he didn't give me his name. He told me "Surprise! – you're going to conceive and give birth to a son! And as for you 'Be sure that you don't drink wine or anything intoxicating and don't eat anything unclean', 'because the young man will be a Nazirite dedicated to God from inside the womb until the day he dies.'" – Judges 13:6-7

She relied on the power of God:

Monoah asked the Angel of the Lord "What's your name, because when what you've said happens, we'll glorify you?" The Angel of the Lord answered him, "Why are you asking this about my name? It's Wonderful!" So Manoah prepared a young goat and a grain offering and offered it on a boulder to the Lord, who kept on performing miracles while Monoah and wife watched continually. When the burnt offering was engulfed in flame that come from the altar, while Monoah and his wife observed this they collapsed on their face to the ground. – Judge 13:9-20

She was confident:

Then Monoah told his wife, "We're going to die for sure because we've seen God!" But his wife replied to him "If the Lord had intended to kill us, he wouldn't have accepted a burnt and a grain offering from us, and he wouldn't have shown us all these things, and he wouldn't have permitted us to hear things like this, now would he?" Later on, the woman gave birth to a son and named him Samson. The child grew strong and the Lord blessed him. – Judges 13:17-24

The wife had a lot of confidence she assured her husband that God was wonderful. The wife believed in herself, she believed in the power and the abilities of God that he would bless her son, Samson, as the twelfth Judge of Israel.

Being Confident is:

1. relying on Jesus
2. believing in Jesus
3. believing in ourselves
4. being consistent

Enemies that rob you of your confidence

1. fear
2. unbelief
3. lack of preparation
4. poor self-esteem

Seal It with a Prayer

Lord give me the confident to know who I am, to walk proudly, to talk softly, to stand firmly and to know that you're with me every step of the way. In the Name of Jesus Amen

Name it and Claim it...

Pray this month about things that God can teach you to be more confident in.... Then claim it, believe it and trust God for it. Stand back and watch Jesus do it.

Author's Reflection

Confidence

Faith gives me the courage to face today's battles with confidence and tomorrow's uncertainty with cheerful hope. ~ Anon

Many of years ago, I remember being unemployed, not knowing how I was going to pay mortgage, buy food, pay to keep gas & electric on, it was very difficult. I felt very depressed going on interview after interview.

My confidence level was very low. I drank alcohol a lot, cried a lot and asked God why me out of all of my sibling, why do I always have to go through?

Then one day as I was going through my petty party the Lord said "Those who are last will be first and those who are first will be last". Jesus said to me "I am taking you through this part of your life so that you can be the stronger sibling. When times are hard for the other sibling, you will be able to guide them through those hard times." In other words suck it up! God gave me the confidence I needed to go on more interviews knowing that I am just as good as or even better than the person sitting across from me. I also learned that I was an asset to the company more than they were an asset to me. If that particular company did not choose me than that position wasn't for me. I kept going on interviews until God places me in a position that's right for me. From that moment on my confidence allowed me to shine on every interview. In Christ Jesus Name Amen (It's done!)

The Lord is a stronghold for the oppressed, a stronghold in times of trouble. ~Psalms 9:9

God's Single Sisters Newsletter

Verses and Scriptures - July Volume 13

Women of Excellency

Excellence-contempt, resourceful, trustworthy, confidence, wisdom, strength, beauty, fineness, distinction, quality, merit

Strength
Exodus. 15:2
Psalms 18:2, 27:1, 28:7, 29:11, 33:16, 29:13, 46:1, 73:26, 81:1, 96:6, 138:13
Isaiah 12:2, 25:4
Judges 5:21
1 Samuel 2:9, 15:29
Job 9:19, 12:13
Proverbs. 10:29
Ecclesiastes 9:16
Luke 1:51
Romans 5:6

God's Powers
Our Loving God is always near; forever by our side; he'll bring us comfort in our fear and place that will abide.

When we trust the power of God, His place keeps us from panic.

They feared exceedingly and said to one another "Who this can be, that even the wind and the sea obey Him!" - Mark 4:41

God's Leading
He does not lead me year by year not even day by day; but step by step my path unfolds; my Lord directs my way—Ryberg

A man's heart plans his way but the Lord directs his steps.-Proverbs 16:9
Instead you ought to say "If the Lord wills, we shall live and do this or that" - James 4:15

The Psalmist Says ♫

I lift up my eyes to the hills where does my help come from? My help (strength) comes from the Lord, the maker of heaven and earth—121:1-2

All about You.......
Name five things that make you strong.

1.

2.

3.

4.

5.

In Christ Jesus Name

Women of The Bible

Merab mean– increase
King Saul's daughter and Saul said to David "Behold my elder daughter Merah her will I give thee to wife; only be thou valiant for me and fight the Lord's battles. But it came to pass at the tune when Merab Saul's daughter should have been given to David that she was given unto Adriel the Meholathite to wife.—1 Samuel 18:17-19

Michal mean—rivulet or who is like Jehovah?
Now Saul's daughter Michal was in love with David, and when they told Saul about it, he was pleased. "I will give her to him," he thought, "so that she may be a snare to him and so that the hand of the Philistines may be against him." So Saul said to David, "Now you have a second opportunity to become my son-in-law." -1 Samuel 18:20-21

Abigail— mean father (i.e. "leader") of the dance or "of joy"
Nabal's wife. She was a woman of good understanding and of a beautiful countenance; but the man was churlish and evil in his doings; and he was of the house of Caleb. And Abigail hasted, and arose, and rode upon an ass, with five damsels of hers that went after her; and she went after the messengers of David and became his wife. -1 Samuel 25:3-18

Women of Courage

Have I not commanded you? Be strong and courageous. Do not be frightened, and do not be dismayed, for the Lord your God is with you wherever you go." – Joshua 1:9

Calm – do not be angry or upset, stay calm

Observe – be watchful and always listen carefully, you can always learn something

Up – don't look down, be direct, and use eye to eye contact

Remove – all doubts and fears

Abilities – access your powers, skills and motivations

Get – ready to bring forth your visions and ministries

Excited – celebrate your accomplishments

Women of Excellence – Strength

Strength is the quality or state of being strong in particular. A good or beneficial quality or attribute of a person or thing.

Abigail was the wife of Nabal. After Nabal's death she became David's second wife.

The man's name was Nabal and his wife's name was Abigail. The woman was intelligent and beautiful while the man was harsh and wicked in his dealings. He was a descendant of Caleb. While David was in the wilderness, he heard that Nabal was shearing his sheep. David sent ten young men, saying to the young men, "Go up to Carmel, find Nabal, and greet him in my name. Then say, 'May you live long. Peace to you peace to your family and peace to all you have. Now, I've heard that the sheep shearers have been with us. We didn't harm them, and they didn't miss anything all the time they were in Carmel. Ask your young men and they'll tell you. Therefore, let my young men find favor with you since we come on a special day. Please give whatever you have available to your servant and to your son David'". – 1 Samuel 25:4-8

Nabal answered David's servants: "Who is David? Who is this son of Jesse? There are many servants today who are breaking away from their masters. Should I take my food, my water, and my meat I've slaughtered from my shearers and give it to men who come from who knows where?" David's men turned and went back and told David everything. David told his men, "Put on your swords" they put on their swords, and David put on his sword. Then about 400 men followed David, while 200 stayed with the supplies.

She had strength in her reaction and thinking:

Now, one of the young men told Nabal's wife Abigail: "Look, David sent messengers from the wilderness to greet our lord, but he screamed insults at them. The men were very good to us. - 1 Samuel 25:14-15

Now, be aware of this and consider what you should do. Calamity is being planned against our master and against his entire household. He's such a worthless person that no one can talk to him." – 1 Samuel 25:17

Abigail quickly took 200 loaves of bread, two skins of wine, five butchered sheep, five measures of roasted grain, 100 bunches of raisins, and 200 fig cakes and loaded them on donkeys. She told her young men, "Go ahead of me, I'll be coming right behind you." But she said nothing to her husband Nabal. She was riding on the donkey and as she went down a protected part of the mountain, David was there with his men, coming down to meet her, and she went toward them. – 1 Samuel 25:18-20

She had strength in her approach:

When Abigail saw David, she quickly got down from the donkey and fell on her face before David, prostrating herself on the ground. She fell at his feet and pleaded, "Your majesty, let the guilt be on me alone, and please let your servant speak to you." Listen to the words of your servant. Please, your majesty, don't pay attention to this worthless man Nabal, for he's just like his name. Nabal is his name and folly is his constant companion. But I, your servant didn't see your majesty's young men whom you sent. - 1 Samuel 25:23-24

She had strength in her judgment:

David told Abigail, "Blessed be the Lord God of Israel, who sent you to meet me today. Blessed be your good judgment, and blessed be you, who today stopped me from shedding blood and delivering myself by my own actions. For as surely as the Lord God of Israel lives, the one who restrained me from harming you—indeed, had you not quickly come to meet me, by dawn there wouldn't be a single male left to Nabal." David took from her what she had brought him and told her, "Go up to your house in peace. Look, I've heard your request and will grant it."- 1 Samuel 25:32-35

She had strength in her boldness:

Abigail returned to Nabal, and he was there in his house holding a festival like the festival of a king. Nabal's heart was glad, and he was very drunk, so she didn't tell him anything at all until morning. After Nabal became sober the next morning, his wife told him all that had happened. Nabal's heart failed and he became paralyzed. About ten days later the Lord struck Nabal, and he died. - 1 Samuel 25:36-38

Abigail couldn't afford to ponder or be afraid because so many lives were in danger. She showed strength and compassion to those who were weak and afraid. She would have made a wonderful leader.

Strong is:
1. being quiet
2. trusting
3. remembering
4. understanding
5. submitting
6. being calm

Enemies that rob you of your strength
1. un-confessed sin
2. un-forgiveness
3. fear

4. anger
5. discouragement
6. self-centeredness
7. anxiety
8. neglecting

Seal It with a Prayer
Lord give me the strength to do the things I need to do and the strength not to do the things I should not be doing. In Christ Jesus Name Amen.

Name it and Claim it...
Pray this month that God gives you the strength to overcome your weaknesses. Claim it, believe it and trust God for it. Stand back and watch God do it.

Author's Reflection

Strength

Strength is born in deep silence of long-suffering hearts not amid Joy. ~ Unknown

My weakness was learning to say no, was not in my vocabulary. Yes, sometimes can be a word that make people take advantage of you. I wanted to say no to my children and I did on occasions but I really did not mean it. I would always give in, my daughter took advantage of the word yes. I would tell her "no" then minutes later say go ahead, that wasn't good parenting. In my younger years I would say "no" to sex but somehow I still gave in, I just should have said yes, morally, this was not good. In the beginning years of my career I would say yes to things that was asked of me, for example: my co-workers who did not feel like talking on the phone to a client or business calls, would say to me "Tell whoever it is on the phone that I'm in a meeting or I have someone in my office". Not true! It was their responsibility to answer that call. As I became older and God strengthen me in that area of saying no, I learned to let my nay be nay and yea be yea, saying no to my children and meaning it, saying no I really don't have time right now, I'm doing something for me today. I learn to say to the caller on the phone at work, "May I take a message, and he/she will call you right back". I learn to be as smart as a serpent but gentle as a dove. In Christ Jesus Name Amen.

My flesh and my heart may fail, but God is the strength of my heart and my portion forever ~ Psalms 73:26

God's Single Sisters Newsletter

Verses and Scriptures - August Volume 14

Women of Excellency

Excellence—contempt, resourceful, trustworthy, confidence, wisdom, strength, beauty, fineness, distinction, quality, merit

Distinction (Difference)
1 Corthinians. 14-17

Beautiful Feet
Christ has no hands but our hands to do His work today; He has no feet but our feet to lead men in His way; He has no tongue but our tongue to tell men how He died; He has no help but our help to bring them to His side—Flint

What Do You Believe
Lord, let me be a shining light in all I say and do that your great love displayed in me may lead someone to You.—Sper

The next person you meet may need to meet Christ. The Lord God has given me the tongue of the learned, that I should know how to speak a word in season to him who is weary.-Isaiah 50:4

The Psalmist Says ♫

I love you, O'Lord my strength. The Lord is my rock, my fortress and my deliverer; my God is my rock in whom I take refuge. He is my hour of my salvation my stronghold. I called to the Lord who is worthy of praise, and I am saved from my enemies - 18:1-3

All about You.......
Name five things about yourself that is distinct (different).

1.

2.

3.

4.

5.
In Christ Jesus

Women of the Bible

Bathsheba mean – daughter of oath, or of seven:
Daughter of Eliam, wife of Uriah. David committed adultery with her. The child conceived through adultery died. After her husband was slain, she become David's wife and Solomon's mother. 2 Samuel 11:2

Tamar mean—palm
A daughter of David, whom Amnon shamefully outraged and afterwards "hated exceedingly," thereby illustrating the law of human nature noticed even by the heathen. -2 Samuel. 13:1-32

Taphath mean—A drop ("distillation; drop of myrrh; stacte i.e., myrrh flowing spontaneously; a drop")
A daughter of King Solomon. She was married to Ben-Abinadab, one of Solomon's twelve district governors over Israel who served in Dor. It was district governor's duty to supply provision to the King and his royal household.— 1 Kings 4:7

Poem for the Month

Beauty of a Woman
The beauty of a woman, isn't in the clothes she wears, the figure that she carries, or the way she combs her hair. The beauty of a woman, must be seen in her eyes, because that's the door way to her heart, the place where love resides. The beauty of a woman, isn't in a facial mole, but true beauty in a woman, is reflected by her soul. It's the caring that she cares to give, the passion that she shows. The beauty of a woman, with passing years, only grows.—Anon

Women of Excellence – Beauty
Beauty – *a combination of qualities, such as shape, color, or form that pleases the aesthetic senses, especially the sight.*

Beautiful - *pleasing the senses or mind aesthetically. Of a very high standard; excellent.*

Sarah – Royalty/Princess Heart
Sarai was her birth name. She was half-sister to Abram. She was the daughter of Terah. Sarah was very beautiful. Sarai was admired because of her beauty, and she was about to become a princess to the Pharaoh but God said no to the Pharaoh you can't have her that Abram wife and that's his princess. – Genesis 12:10-20

God confirmed his covenant with Abram at age ninety-nine from that covenant he named Abram - Abraham meaning father of all nations and named Sarai – Sarah meaning mother of all nations. Sarah was no longer Abraham's princess alone now she was the nation's princess – Genesis 17:1-17

Rachel – Submissive Heart
Now Labon had two daughters; the name of the older was Leah, and the name of the younger was Rachel. Leah had weak eyes, but Rachel was lovely in form and beautiful. - Genesis 29:16

Rachael was a very beautiful woman, Jacob's princess, he loved her very much. She knew that Jacob loved her; she knew that he worked fourteen years so that she could become his wife, and he could continue loving her for the rest of their lives.

Hannah – Praying Heart
Hannah was born from Ramathaim Zophim, she was the wife of Elkanah a Zuphite from the hill country of Ephraim. She was Samuel's mother. Hannah was a beautiful woman, she was a graceful woman, she was kind, and she had favor in God's eyes.

So Hannah ate. Then she pulled herself together, slipped away quietly, and entered the sanctuary. The priest Eli was on duty at the entrance to God's Temple in the customary seat. Crushed in soul, Hannah prayed to God and cried and cried—inconsolably.

Then she made a vow: Oh, God-of-the-Angel-Armies, If you'll take a good, hard look at my pain, If you'll quit neglecting me and go into action for me by giving me a son, I'll give him completely, unreservedly to you. I'll set him apart for a life of holy discipline.—
1 Samuel 1:9-11

Bathsheba – Obeying Heart
Bathsheba was very beautiful, she was the daughter of Elaim and the wife of Uriah her first husband. David was her second husband after Uriah death. Her first child was conceived in an adultery relationship the child died. Her second child was named Solomon.

David got up from his couch and was walking around on the roof of the royal palace. From there he watched a woman taking a bath, and she was very beautiful to look at. David sent word to inquire about her, and someone told him, "This is Eliam's daughter Bathsheba, the wife of Uriah the Hittite, isn't it?" So David sent some messengers, took her from her home, and she went to him, and he had sex with her. -1 Samuel 11:2-4

Esther – Peaceful Heart
Hadasshah or Esther, the daughter of Mordecai's uncle, she had neither a mother nor father, so Mordecai raised her as his own daughter. She was very lovely and beautiful to look at.

So when the king's order and his edict were proclaimed, and when many young women were gathered in Susa the citadel in custody of Hegai, Esther also was taken into the king's palace and put in custody of Hegai, who had charge of the women. And the young woman pleased him and won his favor. And he quickly provided her with her cosmetics and her portion of food, and with seven chosen young women from the king's palace, and advanced her and her young women to the best place in the harem. - Esther 2:8-9

Beauty is not good looks, or a contest of who looks better, or movie stars or fashion models. Beauty are traits that are nurtured within our hearts.

Paul says that we are to be clothed in:
>   compassion
>   kindness
>   humility
>   gentleness
>   patience
>   forbearance

Seal It with a Prayer

Lord when I feel fat and ugly and very distance about myself, when I am around people who I feel are more distinguish, remind me that you see the Beauty in me and remind me that I am a woman of beauty inside and out, because I am wonderfully made and fearfully made and marvelous are your works.—In Christ Jesus Name Amen

Name it and Claim it...

Pray this month that you recognize how distinguish you are in all things. Claim it, believe it and trust God for it. Stand back and watch God do it.

Author's Reflection

Beauty

Beauty is not caused, it is. ~ Emily Dickerson

I remember as a teenager well into my young adult years, being very self-conscious about being heavy, fat, big-boned whatever they want to call it, I was the heaviest of all of my sisters and brothers. During my teen years I was consistently told that I was too heavy and I needed to lose weight. I was teased by my brothers they used to call me "H-R-Fatest Pooh". I was teased by this one neighborhood boy. He was always saying "last one in first to eat." People will never understand the impact on the things that they say even if they feel at the moment that it is good for you. I was ashamed of myself. I was never told that I was beautiful in spite of my weight. I cried a lot and often stayed to myself. I often wrote in my diary, that's where I developed my love for writing, it was a get-away for me. When I was in High School I felt that none of the boys liked me because of my weight. I was a plain looking girl. I decided when I turned eighteen that I would lose the weight so, I joined a weight lost center where they would hypnotized their clients against the food that they liked by reaching their self-conscious minds. Once you were hypnotize from that particular food you enjoyed your desire for that food was gone. Nice concept except the center never taught the nutritional value of being healthy, they never taught exercise techniques. I lost weight from practically starving myself. One day when I was in line registering for college classes, I blacked completely out, when I came around I found myself in the Nurse's office, not knowing what happen, at that point I realized that I was not eating properly; I was eating an apple here and drinking lots of water there, but that wasn't real food. After experiencing my black out I never returned to the center. I taught myself how to diet and exercise losing a good amount of weight. As my daughter became a teen, (she is on the heavy side) I would always encourage her telling her how beautiful she was inside and outside. I would tell her to feel good about herself no matter what people thought. Did I take that advice for myself, No! I was still walking around looking just as plain as I could look. As my daughter got older she encouraged me to wear up to date hair styles and clothes that matched my shoes. That was great and I appreciate her encouragement, but it wasn't until my mid-forties that I realize beauty is not an outward thing. Your hair can be looking neat every day with not a strand out of place, clothes can be looking like all that, which is a good thing but if your inside beauty is out of sort, you're mean and hateful or have no compassion it makes everything look ugly. Inward beauty is what brings the outward beauty out. I looked at my kindness, my compassion and love for others and guess what I felt and looked good "yawl" inside and out. And oh by the way, the neighborhood boy who teased me every day, now he compliments me on my inward beauty as well as outward beauty. In Christ Jesus Name Amen.

God's Single Sisters Newsletter

Verses and Scriptures - September Volume 15

Women of Excellency

Excellence—contempt, resourceful, trustworthy, confidence, wisdom, strength, beauty, fineness, distinction, quality, merit

Trust
Job 13:15, 39:11
Psalms 25:2, 31:6, 55:32, 56:3, 143.8,
118.8, 144:2
Isaiah 50:10
Jeremiah 49:11
Micah 7:5
Nehemiah 1:7
Matthew 27.43
Luke 18:9

Our Refuge and Strength
Trust in God and you will know he can vanquish any foe; simply trust Him day by day, He will be your strength and stay.—D. De Haan

No life is more secure than a life surrendered to God.

Some trust in chariots, and some in horses, but we will remember the name of the Lord our God—Psalm 20:7

Do not worry.....your heavenly Father knows that you need all these things—Matthew 6:31-32

Verses and Scriptures

I don't know about tomorrow, it may bring me poverty; but the One who feeds the sparrow is the One who stands by me.—Stamphill

Worry is a burden God never intended us to bear.

The Psalmist Says 🎵

To you I call, O Lord my rock; do not turn a deaf ear to me. For if you remain silent, I will be like those who have gone down to the pit. Hear my cry for mercy as I call to you for help, as I lift up my hands towards your most Holy place - 28:1-2

All about You.......
Name five things that you try not to worry about......

1.

2.

3.

4.

5.
In Christ Jesus Name

Back To School

Parents have you ever seen a nail that has been bent? Ever try to straighten one? Pretty difficult job, isn't it? These questions are directly related to the growth of our children. Once a child is past the age of twelve or thirteen, whatever "shape" they are in is just like that nail hard to straighten out. As parents, we are given children as a gift from the Lord. Psalm 127 states "Children are a heritage of the Lord: and the fruit of the womb is His reward." If they are given to us by the Lord, then the Lord knows how we should raise them up. Much like the company that make cars they know the appropriate care of the car, the instructions are usually found in the owner's manual. Our children come with an owner's manual also; it's called the Holy Bible, The Word of God. In this manual Jesus tells us "suffer (let) little children come unto me, and forbid them not: for of such is the kingdom of God" – Mark 10:14.

In the book of Proverbs, it is written: "Train up a child in the way he should go" – Proverbs 22:6. Then in John 14:6 Jesus tells us "I am the way". All these admonitions to parents from the Word of God points us toward a good Christian's education. In our culture today, it is very necessary that we let the Creator of the product help to keep it in good running order, don't you agree? Teaching your children about love opens up him/her to receive it and act it out among their peers. Would you rather the "world" trained your children in the way they should go, and then who know which way they will go! Your part in your children receiving a Christian education is vital. So get your children prepared for Sunday school and school if you don't then the "world" will it's real simple... and the choice is yours. Give your children a chance, Give them to Jesus. In the Name of Jesus...Amen – Anon.

Woman of Excellence

But someone will say, "You have faith and I have works." Show me your faith apart from your works, and I will show you my faith by my works. – James 2:18

When God calls us he equips, he enables and provides us for the task ahead.

*Q*uality – your standards and goals of excellence has to shine "put your best foot forward"
*U*nderstand – you will experience some set-backs, don't let it stop you keep it moving
*A*lways – try even if you do not succeed at that moment, keep on trying
*L*earn – from your mistakes
I*d*entify – your visions, your dreams and your ministries
*F*avor – receive God's favor, it's a Blessing
*Y*ours – it's yours, go for it.....

<u>Woman of Excellence – Conclusion</u>
Throughout these series we visited five qualities unique to a woman of excellence:

Resourcefulness – Deborah knew how to be resourceful when prompted with new situation, difficult situation and coping skills.

Trustworthiness – Phoebe, Priscilla and Aquila are prefect examples of trust

Confidence- Manoah's wife (Samson's Mother), had rock solid confidence

Strength - Abigail strength was amazing

Beauty – Sarah, Rachel, Hannah, Bathsheba and Esther were all beautiful, but they also had traits that was nurtured in their hearts

Abigail had all five of these excellent qualities she was resourceful; when the servants come to tell her about what her husband Nabal said to David's men she was right on it, she didn't hesitate, she didn't stop to think, she just loaded up everything that she knew would be a good will gift to please David and his men.

She was trustworthy; because she not only saved her life but saved the lives of all the servants and their families.

She had confidence; presenting David and his men with the gifts and speaking to David intellectually would protect her and the servants.

Her strength was amazing; how she confronted David and Nabil was outstanding, Abigail didn't know if she was going to live or die, but she walked on faith, plus she was beautiful which gave her some "brownie" point.

Becoming a Woman of Excellence:
- allow yourself to love yourself
- look at yourself honestly
- don't condemn yourself
- have an attitude of love and forgiveness toward others
- do things that will make you like yourself
- choose realist goals
- seek God
- determine to use your abilities and gifts for the building of others
- seek out friends who will build you up
- trust God to mold you into the person he wants you to be
- thank God for his endless, limitless love for you
- thank God for the future He has prepared for you

Seal It with a Prayer

Father teach me to be content with the things you have given me. Help me to be resourceful to obtain the things I need. Trustworthy to the people you send across my feet and confident that anything I put my mind too I can do it. Give me wisdom to get it done and strength while doing it. Give me the confident to see how beautiful I am inside and out. In the Name of Jesus. Amen

Name it and Claim It...

Pray this month about learning how to trust God in everything you do. Then claim it, believe it and trust God for it. Stand back and watch God do it.

Author's Reflection

Trust

Help us to still trust you when we can't see you, when we can't hear you, and when our prayers seem to go unanswered. Help us to trust you in the darkness even more than we do in the light –Anon

I lost the house that I was buying in 2001, living there for seven years was very hard to accept. It felt like I was walking with my eyes closed "yawl", very often I cried so hard until I could not see. Several of the Sisters at church ministered and prayed with me but noone could bring me out except the Lord. I felt alone, a disappointment to my children, and I felt that God was nowhere to be found that he didn't hear my cries. In the process of moving I had to leave my dogs to be cared for by someone that I did even know, the lady I left my animals with, sold my dogs to someone else in exchange for drugs, some of my furniture was trashed it seems like everything was coming against me. My daughter started rebelling, because she had to leave a place where she was rooted, and she had to leave her friends. I had a one-year old whose father was never there from conception. And then there's my family well let just say, sometimes you can get more help from, strangers. In this season of my life and the storm that was ahead, I had to learn to Trust on the Lord. I had to learn to endure, I had to learn where my strength came from I had to learn to suck it up. After all of this I continued reading different scriptures to strengthen me daily, praying every night, and thanking God for giving me and my family a new start each day. In Christ Jesus Name

He did not hide his face from me, but heard when I cried to him – Psalm 22:24

Discovering Your Ministries
The Series
October – December

God's Single Sisters Newsletter

Verses and Scriptures - October Volume 16

Discovering Your Ministries

Minister—attend, tend, help

Attend
Psalms 17:1, 55:2
Proverbs 4:1
1 Corinthians 7:35
1 Timothy 4:13

Too Old?

In the strength of the Lord let me labor and pray. Let me watch as a winner of souls; that bright stars may be mine in the glorious day, when His praise like the sea-billow rolls.—Hewitt

No one is too old to be witness for Christ. You are the light of the world.—Matthews 5:14

Be Coachable
Oh, it's hard to learn the lesson as we pass beneath the rod, that the sunshine and the shadow serve alike the will of God. God's work in us isn't over when we receive Christ it has just begun. - Unknown

I have learned in whatever state I am, to be content.—Philippians 4:11

Ecclesiastes Says 📖

Guard your steps when you go to the house of God. Go near to listen rather than to offer the sacrifice of fools, who do not know that they do wrong. - 5:1

All about You.......
Name five things that you should be attentive too...

1.

2.

3.

4.

5.
In Christ Jesus Name

Women of the Bible

Basemeth/Basmath/Basmathe mean—fragrant or perfumed
Mention three times in the bible:

One of the wives of Esau, a daughter of Elon, the Hittite - Genesis 26:34

Another wife of Esau, a daughter of Ishmael and a sister of Nebaioth. - Genesis 36:3,4,10,13,17 and Genesis 28:9

The daughter of Solomon, and wife of Ahimaaz, a commissariat-officer in the service of Solomon - 1 Kings 4:15

Tahpenes/Taph-hanes mean— the head of the age
The wife of Pharaoh, who gave her sister in marriage to Hadad the Edomite. When this sister, whose name is not given, died, probably in childbirth, Tahpenes became the foster mother of her only son, Genubath, and brought him up as her own child. - 1 Kings 11:19,20

Zeruah mean— Leprous or Stricken
Mother of Jeroboam, the first king of the ten tribes—1 Kings 11:26

Rejoice
Rejoice in the Lord always; again I will say, Rejoice. - Philippians 4:4

*R*eceive – your gifts and your blessings

*E*late – be ecstatically happy because it comes from God

*J*oy - no one should be allowed to take it

*O*riginal – your gifts and blessings is not a carbon copy, it's yours

*I*mportant – be humble with your blessings and pass it on

*C*elebrate – the goodness of God

*E*xcited – there's more to come

Discovering Your Ministries –Women Ministry a Brief History
Ministry *– the work or vocation of a minister of religion*
Likewise, older women are to show their reverence for God by their behavior. They are not to be gossips or addicted to alcohol, but to be examples of goodness. They should encourage the younger women to love their husbands, to love their children, to be sensible and pure, to manage their households, to be kind, and to submit themselves to their husbands. Otherwise, the word of God may be discredited – Titus 2:3-5

Ordination mean - formal recognition and commissioning of a person for ministerial authority and responsibility. The first woman was ordained in 1853. Wesleyam Methodist ordain a woman in 1861, the Pentecostal church ordain a woman 1909, the Assemblies of God ordained women starting in 1914, the United Methodist Church and Presbyterian churches in the United States have been ordaining women since 1914, the Lutheran church in America since 1970 and the Episcopal church since 1977. Baptist groups have ordained women since the 1600s although most Baptist churches rejected the idea.

Deaconess – the ministry of a deaconess is in modern times a non-ordained ministry. The word comes from a Greek word, diakonos meaning a servant or helper. Deaconess roots back in the time of Jesus Christ through the present.

Mission – women ministry centers on meeting the needs of women in the Christian Churches. The word ministry comes from the Greek word diakned which means to serve. Women ministry exist to serve women and teach them how to serve others. Women ministries have increased in the past decade, especially in the Christian church. Women ministries in the church are often voluntary, member of the congregation or church staff.

- The first group of women to form a ministry was the Woman's Missionary. Women in 1888 served as an auxiliary branch to the Southern Baptist Convention. The primary purpose of this organization was to educate and inspire women in Christian Mission work as well as connecting women with different outreach opportunities.
- Senior Women's Mission Society – March 1895 – purpose giving aide
- Valley Ladies Circle – July, 1909 – purpose bible study work and prayer
- Jr. Women Ministry Society – January 1920 – purpose bible study, prayer and mission
- Missionary Guild – 1948 - purpose better understanding of the missionary objectives of the boards domestic and foreign missions

Seal It with a Prayer

Lord teach me as I get older to be more coachable in helping people understand things and to be more attentive to their needs. In Christ Jesus Name Amen.

Name it and Claim It...

Pray this month that God gives you the understanding to be more coachable and attentive to others. Claim it, believe it and stand back and watch God do it.

Author's Reflection

Attend

An unmarried woman or virgin is concern about the Lord's affairs: Her aim is to be devoted to the Lord in both body and spirit. But a married woman is concerned about the affairs of this world – how she can please her husband. I am saying this for your own good not to restrict you, but that you may live in a right way in undivided devotion to the Lord. A woman is bound to her husband as long as he lives, but if her husband dies, she is free to marry anyone she wishes, but he must belong to the Lord. In my judgment, she is happier if she stays as she is – and I think that I too have the Spirit of God. 1 Corinthians 7:34-40.

God's Single Sisters
Newsletter

Verses and Scriptures -November Volume 17

Discovering Your Ministries
Minister—attend, tend, help

<u>Tend</u>
Prov. 11:19, 14:23, 19:23, 21:5

<u>Harvest Home</u>
Even so, Lord, quickly come to the final harvest-home: Gather thus thy People in free from sorrow, free from sin; there, forever purified, in thy presence to abide: Come, with all thine angels, come raise the glorious harvest-home. - Unknown

<u>Get In the Game</u>
Start where you are in serving the Lord, claim His sure promise and trust in His Word; God simply asks you to do what you can, He'll use your efforts to further His plan.—Anon

To this end I also labor, striving according to His working which works in me mightily. —Colossians 1:29

Ecclesiastes Says 📖
The quiet words of the wise are more to be needed then the shouts of a ruler of fools. Wisdom is better than weapons of war, but one sinner destroys much good—9:17

All about You.......
Name five things about yourself that's decent.
1.
2.
3.
4.
5.
In Christ Jesus Name

Giving Thanks

"Therefore I tell you, do not be anxious about your life, what you will eat or what you will drink, nor about your body, what you will put on. Is not life more than food, and the body more than clothing? Look at the birds of the air: they neither sow nor reap nor gather into barns, and yet your heavenly Father feeds them. Are you not of more value than they? And which of you by being anxious can add a single hour to his span of life? And why are you anxious about clothing? Consider the lilies of the field, how they grow: they neither toil nor spin, yet I tell you, even Solomon in all his glory was not arrayed like one of these. – Matthews 6:25-34

Author's Reflection

We are about to embark on another Thanksgiving and Christmas holidays. I would like to stop and reflection on Thanksgiving. When I was a child Thanksgiving was an exciting time of the year because of the school break, good food and the gathering of people and relatives that we usually do not get to see that often during the year. As I became an adult and started to walk with God, I view thanksgiving as an everyday praise. I thank God for my children's health and safety, my family's health and safety. I thank God that I am surrounded by such wonderfully Sisters in my immediate family, and at work. Sisters who God have allowed to cross my path, whether it's my siblings or my friends, each one have been my strength this year. Whether it was negative or positive I have embraced their advice, their help, their prayers and certainly their Godly love and it has helped me to go on and do what I have to do. Jesus I thank you for allowing me to be the author of God's Single Sisters Newsletter. It has been a joy to minister through this newsletter. I am thankful to you Lord for the small storms and the big victories, it has kept me going, pushing forward and closer toward the goals in Christ Jesus Name. Lord I want to thank you for the most important thing which is YOU JESUS! I pray that everyone have a very nice and peaceful Thanksgiving. In Christ Jesus Name Amen!

Discovering Your Ministries –Women Ministry (Biblical)
Ministry – *the work or vocation of a minister of religion*

I am reminded of your sincere faith, which first existed in your grandmother Lois and your mother Eunice, and I am convinced that this faith also exists in you. – 2 Timothy 1:5

Ministries......
- Mary – Compassion – She anointed Jesus' feet
- Maratha – Hospitality – She prepared food for Jesus
- Debra – Prophetess, Judge and Song writer

- Lydia – Hospitality, business woman and prayer warrior. Known as the purple lady, she made dye and dyed her clothes purple she also prayed daily at the river, as well as housed missionaries
- Phoebe – Deaconess at a church in Cenchrea
- Pricilla and Aquilla – faithful worker for Paul and the church
- Miriam – was the first women Prophetess and singer
- Hannah- poetess, prophetess and singer

Seal It with a Prayer

Lord on this Day of Thanks, remind me of the things I should be thanking you for things you have blessed me with leading up to this day. In Christ Jesus Name Amen.

Name it and Claim it.......

Pray this month to be diligent about thanking God for everything not only for this day but for every day. Claim it, believe it, and trust God for it, stand back and watch God do it...

Author's Reflection

Intentions (Lending a Helping Hand)

Lord I cannot claim to be living on higher grounds than others. When I stop to lend a lifting hand, show me that I can reach across ~ Anon

One day on my lunch break, I walked to Lexington Market to get a sandwich. I didn't have any money but I had food stamps. As I was standing in line at the counter waiting to order, a lady come up to me and asked me if I could spare some change, she said she was hungry. I said to her "Ms. I don't have any money, but I can buy you something with my stamps." I purchased some lunch meats; ham, brunsweger and turkey and gave it to the lady. She thanked me over and over. She said she was going to take the food home. Before leaving, she said to me "I am so grateful thank you." I said to her "no problem, because God feeds me every day, as she turned to leave I said to her "have a blessed rest of the day." I never saw that woman again, but I was so glad that I was there to give a leading hand

If a brother or sister naked and lacks daily food, and one of you says to them "Go in peace keep warm and eat your fill," and yet you do not supply their bodily needs, what is the good of that ~ James 2:15-16

God's Single Sisters Newsletter

Verses and Scriptures - December Volume 18

Discovering Your Ministries

Minister - attend, tend, and help

<u>Help</u>
Genesis 2:18
Job 6:13
Psalms 33:20, 46:1, 121:1
Matthew 15:25
2 Corinthians 1:11

<u>Drinkin' From My Saucer</u>
I've never made a fortune and it's prob'ly too late now; But I don't worry about that much, I'm happy anyhow! And as I go along life's way reapin' better then I sowed. I'm drinkin' from my saucer, because my cup has over flowed! Haven't got a lot of riches, and sometimes the going's tough' but I've got loving ones around me, and that makes me rich enough! I thank God for His blessings and the mercies He's bestowed. I'm drinkin' from my saucer, cause my cup has over flowed! I member times when things went wrong, my faith wore somewhat thin; but all at once the dark clouds broke and light peeped through again. So, Lord, help me not to grip about tough rows I've hoed, I'm drinkin' from my saucer, cause my cup has over flowed! If God give me strength and courage when the way grows steep and rough, I'll not ask for other blessings; I'm already blessed enough! May I never be too busy to help other bear their load I'll keep drinkin from my saucers, cause my cup has overflowed—Jimmy Dean

<u>Blue Christmas</u>
Whenever darkness grips your soul and you are tempted to despair, remember Christ's unfailing love and trust His faithful tender care.—Sper

Ecclesiastes Says 📖
Whatever is has already been and what will be had been before and God will call the past to account.—3:15

All about You.......
Name five things you can do for yourself this Holiday.
1.
2.
3.
4.
5.
In Christ Jesus Name

Author's Reflection

And the angel came in unto her, and said, Hail, thou that art highly favored, the Lord is with thee; and when she saw him, she was troubled at his saying, and cast in her mind what manner of salutation this should be. And the angel said unto her Fear not, Mary; for thou hast found favor with God. And, behold, thou shalt conceive in thy womb, and bring forth a son, and shalt call his name Jesus. - Luke 1:28-31

Mothers we are highly favored in God's eyesight. He has given us a precious gift and that gift is the ability to give life through birth. So this Christmas give the ultimate gift, hug your children, and tell your children that you love them, that they matter and that you appreciate them. Give them back the gift that God have given you that is the Gift of Life. In Christ Jesus Name Amen. Have a blessed, safe, happy and peaceful Holy Day.

Prevail

He said: "Listen, King Jehoshaphat and all who live in Judah and Jerusalem! This is what the Lord says to you: 'Do not be afraid or discouraged because of this vast army. For the battle is not yours, but God's." - 2 Chronicles 20:15

*P*atience – be patient wait on God

*R*ealistic – while you're waiting see things as they real are

*E*ager – do not rush things, let God handle it

*V*ictory – get ready your battle is almost over

*A*llow – yourself to heal, rest and relax

*I*nspire – be creative, do something for yourself

*L*oosen – up and release, God got your back

Discovering Your Ministries –Your Spiritual Gifts
***Ministry** – the work or vocation of a minister of religion*

Now there are varieties of gifts, but the same Spirit, and there are varieties of ministries, but the same Lord. There are varieties of results, but it is the same God who produces all the results in everyone. To each person has been given the ability to manifest the Spirit for the common good. To one has been given a message of wisdom by the Spirit; to another the ability to speak with knowledge according to the same Spirit; to another faith by the same Spirit; to another gifts of healing by that one Spirit; to another miraculous results; to another prophecy; to another the ability to distinguish between spirits; to another various kinds of languages; and to another the interpretation of languages. But one and the same Spirit produces all these results and gives what he wants to each person. - 1 Corinthians 12:4-11

We all know that a ministry is a gift from God something that we do not get to pick on our own. I believe that God give gifts to those he knows that are passion, patience with and good at, it's just like being pregnant, when we conceive our gifts or ministries, it's the beginning of our pregnancy we have to carry that idea or vision to term, then we have to go through the labor pains, labor pains of developing our ministry which sometimes bring disappointments, let-downs and discouragements. But then here comes the birth, now it's really a reality, now we have to name our baby, my baby name is God's Single Sisters Newsletter my firstborn, long name is it, then we have to look at our ministry/our baby's characters (what our ministries about and the purpose of it). My purpose is encouraging Single Mothers through my newsletters. Then we have to raise it, love our ministry, be compassion and be committed. My second born was teaching computer classes, my purpose was to help adults and young adults to become job ready and help our seniors to learn and feel comfortable with computers. While we are discovering our gifts and ministries we should always keep it in prayer remembering our first purpose is to glorify the Kingdom of God, let the Holy Spirit guide us and allow Jesus to mature our gifts or ministries. Our ministries and gifts belong to us, embrace it. In Christ Jesus Name Amen.

Seal It with a Prayer

Lord this Christmas remind me that someone else cup was running over, and they shared it with me. Now my cup runs over and I need to share with someone. In Christ Jesus name. Amen

Name it and Claim it...

This month pray and ask God to teach you how to pour some blessing into someone's life so their cup can run over. Claim it, believe it and trust God for it. Stand back and watch God do it...

Author's Reflection

Help Me Lord!

Help me to remember God that the best way out is always through your guidance.
In the past God has always given me guidance even when I really did not understand or even know. When I cried out, his guidance and strength was right there helping me to speak and understand. I've always had financial difficulties with paying my rent, every time I get on a schedule here comes a new problem. I always had to play catch-up because I

had this difficulty, I would have to seek informational services, agencies, relatives and friends. God sends a lot of people across my feet to assist me, these people would also give me important resources which enabled me to gain knowledge in helping someone else.

Though I walk in the midst of trouble, you preserve me against the wrath of my enemies; you stretch out your hand and your right hand delivers me – Psalms 138:7

Newsletter III
January – December

Restore – He restoreth my soul: he leadeth me in the paths of righteousness for his name's sake. – Psalms 23:3

The Single Life
The Series
January – April

God's Single Sisters
Newsletter

Verses and Scriptures - January Volume 19

The Single Life

Single-alone, private, sociable

<u>Alone</u>
Numbers 11:14
Deuteronomy 1:9
1 King 11:29
Psalms 136
Matthew 4:4, 18:5

<u>Pray, Pursue and Praise</u>
I must put my relationship With you, O Lord, I pray, above what may distract me from time spent with you each day.—Sper

God pursues us in our restlessness, receives us in our sinfulness, holds us in our brokenness—Scotty Smith

Because you're loving kindness is better than life, my lips shall praise You.—Psalms 63:3

They entered into an oath to walk in God's law and to observe and do all the commandments of the LORD our Lord- Nehemiah 10:29

Our resolutions needs not be as serious as that, but any resolution to follow God is not a casual promise. Rather, it is a solemn and serious declaration that with the help of the Holy Spirit we can renew every day. - Marvin Williams

Song of Songs Says 🎵

Beloved—like an apple tree among the young men, I delight to sit in his shade, and his fruit is sweet to my taste. He has taken me to the banquet hall, and his banner over me is love. Strengthen me with raisins, refresh me with apples, for I am faint with love. His left arm is under my head and his right arm embraces me. - Song of Songs 2:3-6

All about You....
Name five things that you can do for yourself, to keep from feeling alone.....
1.
2.
3.
4.
5.
In Christ Jesus Name

Women of the Bible

Jezebel mean—chaste or where is the Prince? (referring to the heathen false god Baal)
The daughter of Ethbaal, the king of the Zidonians, and the wife of Ahab, the king of the kingdom of Israel - 1 Kings 16:31

Abishag mean—father i.e., given to, error.
This was the name of a beautiful young woman of Shunem. She was chosen to minister to David in his old age, to attempt to nurse him to health and to keep him warm. She appears to have become David's closest attendant. - 1 Kings 1:3-4, 15

Vashti mean—beautiful
The queen of Ahasuerus, who was deposed from her royal dignity because she refused to obey the king when he desired her to appear in the banqueting hall of Shushan the palace -Esther 1:10-12

Esther mean— a star
The queen of Ahasuerus, and heroine of the book that bears her name she was a Jewess named Hadas'sah (the myrtle), but when she entered the royal harem she received the name by which she henceforth became known. - Esther 2:7

New Year
When the New Year dawns, I wish you the strength and serenity of the mountains, the power and flows of the river, the grace and flight of a soaring bird and a New Year filled with new beginnings, new promises, new opportunities, new triumphs and an amazingly successful YOU.—Alexis

Arthur's Reflection

Happy New Year Ladies… My prayer for you is that this year will be a year of "You". A Year knowing who you are emotionally, mentally and socially, a year of discovering who you are spiritually, a year knowing that you are special—loved, fearfully and wonderfully made and marvelous is his works. I pray that we understand that Jesus has given us the power of prayer, and through trust and belief that power is released. I pray that we also discover and embrace the ministries that are inside of us, birthing our babies (ministries) this year. I pray that God sends us that very special "handpicked" husband that we long for and desire. Finally, I pray that all needs be met and that every one of our prayers come to pass. Pamper yourself this year ladies we deserve it. . . . . . May God fully bless you and yours in the renewing of your life.

Seal It with a Prayer

When asked what's my New Year Resolution? I responded: "To do what God wants, when he wants and where he wants me to do it." In Christ Jesus Name Amen.

The Single Life – Loneliness
Single – *relating to a state of being unmarried or uninvolved in a romantic relationship*
Lonely – *unhappy as a result of being without the companion of others*

But seek first the kingdom of God and his righteousness, and all these things will be added to you. – Matthew 6:33

Pray and let Jesus know that you are lonely, but when you pray, please oh please, don't pray "O' God I just want a man, I need a man". If you pray that prayer you might just get a man! Sometimes we get exactly what we pray for. Describe your man in your prayers: God already knows what kind of man, he wants for us, but He also wants to hear from you. God is making your husband while you pray, I believe all things are possible with God for those who believe.

While you Wait....

Delight yourself in the LORD, and he will give you the desires of your heart. Commit your way to the LORD; Trust him, and he will act. Psalms 37:4-5

First, establish a relationship with the LORD, find peace and joy and contentment in him first.

Secondly, ask God to forgive and then read/study the word of God to understand how God wants you to live

Finally, trust God and everything you do and in all situation

"I am the true vine, and my Father is the vine dresser. Every branch in me that does not bear fruit he takes away, and every branch that does bear fruit he prunes so that it may bear more fruit. You are already clean because of the word that I have spoken to you. Abide in me, and I in you. As the branch cannot bear fruit by itself, unless it abides in the vine, neither can you, unless you abide in me. I am the vine; you are the branches. Whoever abides in me and I in him, will bear many fruit; for apart from me you can do nothing. ... – John 15:1-27

We need to recognize that God is God all by himself. Believe in our prayers and take him at his words.

Let your eyes be on the field that they are reaping, and go after them. Have I not charged the young men not to touch you? And when you are thirsty, go to the vessels and drink what the young men have drawn." – Ruth 2:9

Keep yourselves busy, discover your ministry or your gifts, so that you will not be tempted and if you do get tempted seek God face first.

Sometimes I get lonely very lonely as a single mother with two children and two grandchildren. My daughter is 29, granddaughter 12 and grandson 9, my son is 17 with one more year in school at this point in my life, I am ready to share the rest of my life with my prince. It does gets hard sometimes, I get depress and start my pity party, asking God "where is my man, I wish I had a man to help me move mountains and climb hills". But then I think back to the scripture delight, commit and trust, and then I remember this one question do I want to wait for the best that God has for me or do I want to settle for the rest? My answer is the best.

Name it and Claim it...

This month pray and ask God how you can make your New Year better than the Old Year. Claim it, believe it and trust God for it. Stand back and watch God do it.

Author's Reflection

Alone

I am feeling my way in the darkness, God, and it seems I'm going in circles. Yet you have reminded me that by being encircled by your love, with every move in any direction, I go no close to you nor farther either than I already am ~ Anon

As I stated in a previous reflection, I had difficulties with keeping housing, many times I had to pack up and leave my home. Each time I felt like I was in the dark, like I was packing boxes with my eyes close, like I was asleep and I did not want to wake up. I felt so alone. I felt like I was going in circles. Every time I had to move there were things I learned that made me strong, the first time I was evicted from my home I realized that Grace and Mercy is very real, the second time I had to move I realized my drinking had to go, the third time God's Single Sisters Newsletter was born (my ministry), and the fourth time I learn how to choose a house or apartment that I could afford. I also learned how to budget better.

When I processed my difficulties I found out that the God of Grace, Mercy, Deliverance, Blessing and Love, was right there the whole time. I wasn't lonely, I was blessed with God's love I could have been homeless sleeping in the street. Ladies it is always darkest until you see the light. So Ladies if you're going through a storm and it's too dark to see, it's cloudy and raining, STOP! BE QUIET, TAKE A MINUTE, and PROCESS what you're going through and PRAY, slowly you'll be able to see the light. Amen

Even though I walk the darkest Valley, I will fear no evil; for you are with me, your rod and your staff ~ they comfort me. Psalms 23:4

God's Single Sisters Newsletter

Verses and Scriptures - February Volume 20

The Single Life

Single-alone, private, sociable

<u>Private (Secret)</u>
Deuteronomy 25:11, 27:15
Job 11:16, 15:8, 27:15
Psalms 19:12, 44:21, 91:1
Song of Songs 2:14
Isaiah 45:3, 45:19

For God so Lo**V**ed the world
    That He g**A**ve
       His on**L**y
      Begott**E**n
        So**N**
          That whoever
   Believes **I**n Him
    Should **N**ot perish
  But have **E**verlasting life

The more you read the Bible, the more you'll love its Author

<u>A To-Do List</u>
The hidden person of the heart must take priority, because our inner character, determines who we'll be. It's not what you do but who you are that's most important. The fruit of the spirit is love, joy, peace, long suffering, kindness, goodness, and faithfulness.-Galatians 5:22

Song of Songs Says ♫

My lover has gone down to his garden to the bed of spices to browse in the gardens and to gather lilies. I am his lover's and my lover is mine; he browses among the lilies—Song of Songs 6:2-3

All about You.....
Name five things that you did in secret that needs forgiveness

1.

2.

3.

4.

5.

In Christ Jesus Name

Women of the Bible

Ahlai mean— Oh that, or Jehovah is staying!

A descendant of Judah. Her name appears only twice in Scripture - 1 Chronicle 2:31 and 11:41

Ahlai father was Sheehan who had no sons, but several daughters.

She was a descendant of Perez Judah's older son by Tamar - Matthew 1:3

Aholah or Aholibah mean—she has her own tentor my tent is in her

This was a name used by Ezekiel (23:4,5,36,44) as a symbol of the idolatry of the kingdom is described as a lewd woman, an adulteress, given up to the abominations and idolatries of the Egyptians and Assyrians. Because of crimes, she was carried away in captivity, and ceased to become a kingdom. - Ezekiel. 23:4, 11, 22, 36, 44

Believe

For God so loved the world, that he gave his only Son, that whoever believes in him should not perish but have eternal life. – John 3:16

*B*ible – the book of life

*E*ternal – Gods words are everlasting, abiding and timeless

*L*ove – his love is impossible to measure or calculated

*I*ntroduce – yourself to him he wants to know you and he wants you to know him

*E*nter – into his rest, peace, love, mercy, faith, grace and favor

*V*ery – you'll be exceedingly glad that you met Jesus and built a relationship with him

*E*xcited – get excited you'll never want to turn back

Seal It with a Prayer

Lord things are so busy around me; give me some private time to spend with you. In Christ Jesus Name Amen

The Single Life – Living Together Before Marriage

Single – *relating to a state of being unmarried or uninvolved in a romantic relationship*

But because of the temptation to sexual immorality, each man should have his own wife and each woman her own husband. – 1 Corinthians 7:2

Flee from sexual immorality. Every other sin a person commits is outside the body, but the sexually immoral person sins against his own body. Or do you not know that your body is a temple of the Holy Spirit within you, whom you have from God? You are not your own, for you were bought with a price. So glorify God in your body. – 1 Corinthians 6:18-20

Jesus said to her, "Go, call your husband, and come here." The woman answered him, "I have no husband." Jesus said to her, "You are right in saying, 'I have no husband'; for you have had five husbands, and the one you now have is not your husband. What you have said is true." – John 4:17-18

1. God is the author of marriage, living together is not a good solution.
2. "I want my cake and ice cream too, is old and played out!" Either marry or separate.
3. Living together cause a let of drama.
4. If you have children, it negatively impacts the children which is sending the wrong message.
5. Last but certainly not least of many reasons, if you keep agreeing to marriage postponement, he'll never marry you.

Name it and Claim it...

Pray this month about the things you did in private which became your secret, that needs forgiveness and ask God to forgive you. Claim it, believe it and trust God for it. Stand back and watch God do it

Author's Reflection

The Month of Love

What does love look like? It has hands to help others; feet to hasten the poor and needy, eyes to see misery and want and ears to hear sighs and sorrows. That is what love looks like.

Some holidays are very depressing to some people. The loneliest holiday to some is Valentine's Day "The Love Month." I never forget in February 1995, I lost someone that was very dear to me, my best friend and father of my oldest, my beloved. We were never married, we stay together and love each other for almost twelve years. The year we decided to get married, God called him home. I was devastated, for eight years I grieved and had very sad moments. February was the hardest, Valentine's Day was a very difficult day to get though, I found myself building an emotional wall around me, afraid to love, and to be loved. On the 9th year of going through, I never forget this; I had a dream about Marvin (my finance'). I dreamed that he had on blue jeans and a white shirt and as I stood there with him I began to feel very alive, and he looked at me and said do not worry I'm okay! As I began to cross the street I looked back and extended my hand out to him to come across with me, and he said he could not, he then motioned me too cross alone. He looked good "yawl" fine as ever. But I knew then that he was alright and I had to let go. So on Valentine's Day I decided to have a date with just me and Jesus. The next moring which was Valentine's day, I picked out an all red outfit, from head to toe, I was looking good. When, I arrived to work everybody thought I had a date. I did but no one knew it was with Jesus. That day I listen to my favorite radio station in Baltimore, as I listen to many gospels singers minister to me, I prayed and talked to Jesus in my heart all day. At the end of the work day, I went to a store that sold balloons. I brought me a Valentine's Day card and some balloons. I got off the bus at my stop and stood there for a minute, then I let all the balloons go and it was so amazing, as the balloons went up, all my hurt and grief went along with those balloons, the higher the balloons went the better I felt. I stood there watching the balloons go up higher and higher and it amazed me how the balloons traveled, the wind did not shift the balloons left or right, they just went straight up. I continue to stand there until I could no longer see the balloons. When I walked away I had such a wonderful feeling because I finally let go.

I gave you a new commandment, that you love one another. Just as I have loved you, you also should love one another – John 13:34

God's Single Sisters
Newsletter

Verses and Scriptures - March Volume 21

The Single Life

Single - alone, private, sociable

<u>Sociable (companionable)</u>
Judges 8:2
Haggai 2:3
Mark 4:30

<u>Taking The Cross</u>
Am I a soldier of the cross? A flower of the Lamb? And shall I fear to own His cause or blush to speak His name - Watts

After all that Christ has done for us, how can we do less than give Him our best?

He who does not take his cross and follow after Me is not worthy of Me—Matthew 10:38

<u>Wanted</u>
I'm available for God to Use me, available, if God should choose me; should it be now or then, it doesn't matter when; I want to see lost souls be born again.—Anthony

God has work for all His children, regardless of age or ability. The Lord has need of him—Luke 19:34

Song of Songs Says 🎵

May the wine go straight to my lover, flowing gently over lips and teeth? I belong to my lover and his desire is for me. Come, my lover, let us go to the country side. Let us go to the vine yards to see if the vines have budded. - Song of Songs 7:10-12

All about You....
Name five things that makes you a sociable Christian....
1.

2.

3.

4.

5.

In Christ Jesus Name

Women of the Bible

Bithiah mean— "daughter of Yahweh", daughter of the Lord; worshiper of Jehovah
Bithiah was a "daughter of Pharaoh." She married Mered, a son of Ezra of the family of Judah. 1 Chronicle 4:18

Hammoleketh mean—the queen
The daughter of Machir and sister of Gilead. -1 Chronicle 7:17, 18

<u>Prayer</u>
Do not be anxious about anything, but in everything by prayer and supplication with thanksgiving let your requests be made known to God. – Philippians 4:6

*P*ersonal – talk to Jesus about your feelings, problems, everything

*R*elease – it is good for the soul

*A*nswer – God answers prayer

*Y*ourself – pray for others, not just yourself

*E*very day – pray without ceasing, thanking God for all blessings

*R*eal – be real when you pray Jesus knows all your needs and wants

Seal It with a Prayer

Lord remind me that my work is a sociable ministry not a closet ministry. In Christ Jesus Name Amen

<u>The Single Life – Prepare Yourself</u>
Single *– relating to a state of being unmarried or uninvolved in a romantic relationship*

<u>*Spiritual Preparation*</u> *- Do not be unequally yoked with unbelievers. For what partnership has righteousness with lawlessness? Or what fellowship has light with darkness? –*
2 Corinthians 6:14

When Christians date or marry nonbelievers, they usually experience:
    conflicting interest
    difficulties teaching their children certain values
    different circles of friends.

Mental Preparation - _and be not conformed to this world: but be ye transformed by the renewing of your mind, that ye may prove what is good, and acceptable, and in the perfect will of God.—Romans 12:2_

study the word of God to guide your life
get out of your old habits, get in to some new habits, that means if you're thinking about getting married some of the things you still do and the places you still go, would have to be adjusted.

Physical Preparation - _relating to the body as opposed to the mind, relating to things perceived through the senses as opposed to the mind; tangible or concrete_

become physically fit mind and body
physically exam yourself, are you ready
physically educate yourself read

Financial Preparation - _Wisdom is a shelter as money is a shelter, but the advantage of knowledge is this: Wisdom preserves those who have it._

wisdom – being experience, good judgment
knowledge – managing your money
understanding – considered, tolerant and be patient when it comes to financial difficulties.

Name it and Claim it...

Pray this month that God shows you how to be more sociable in your ministry. Claim it, believe it and trust God for it. Stand back and watch God do it.

Author's Reflection

Sociable (Compassion)

A lonely Coworker, hurting friend, or disappointed family member is hungry for my love and encouragement. How can I offer a blessing in word or action today?

When I first started working at a homeless shelter for Women in 1998, I soon learn that homelessness was real. When I was accepted for the job, the first time I walked through the door, I knew that it would not just be a "job" but a ministry. I knew that God had sent me there to encourage, help, talk to the lonely, the hungry, pray for the depressed whether it was a co-worker, a client or a friend. It has not been an easy job to do, sometimes it became overwhelming but every time I begin to feel like I'm fed up and thoughts of leaving came to mind God said to me "Not yet", so I continued to be sociable with compassion until it's time for my change to go somewhere else and be sociable and compassionate

Above all, clothe yourselves with love which binds everything together in perfect harmony – Colossians 3:14

God's Single Sisters Newsletter

Verses and Scriptures ~ April Volume 22

The Single Life
Single-alone, private, sociable

<u>Separate</u>
Genesis 13:9
Deuteronomy 19:2
Proverb16:28
Matthew 25:32
Romans 8:35

<u>Pornography</u>
The world is passing and the lust of it; but he who does the will of God abides forever – 1 John 2:17

Verses and Scriptures
I am resolved to follow the Savior faithful and true each day; heed what He sayeth do what he willeth – He is the living way – Hartsough

Choose for yourself whom you will serve but as for me and my house hold we will serve the Lord. -Joshua 24:45

Song of Songs Says 🎵
Under the apple tree I aroused you; there your mother conceived you there she who was in labor gave you birth. Place me like a seal over your heart, like a seal on your arm; for love is as strong as death, its jealousy unyielding as the grave, like a might flame – Song of Songs 8:5-6

All about You....
Name five things that you should as a woman of God be separate from
1.
2.
3.

Women of the Bible

Oholah mean - express, surprise or mark
A Samaria woman, oldest of the two sisters who were prostitutes. She gave herself as a prostitute to all the elite of the Assyrians and defiled herself with all the idols of everyone she lusted after— Ezekiel 23:7

Oholihah mean – my tent
Was the youngest sister of Oholah. She too lusted after the Assyrians governors and commanders, Warriors in fall dress, mounted horseman, all handsome young men. – Ezekiel 23:11

Lorhamah – means not loved
She was Hosea's first daughter, a type of Jehovah's temporary rejection of his people. -Hosea 1:6; 2:23

Poem for the Month

The Rose
It's only a tiny rosebud a flower of God's design; but I cannot unfold the petals with these clumsy hand of mine. The secret of unfolding flowers is not known to such so gently, in my hands would fade and die. If I cannot unfold a rose bud this flower of God design, how can I have wisdom to unfold this life of mine? So I'll look to Him for His guidance each step of the pilgrim way. For the pathway that lies before me my heavenly Father knows I'll trust Him to unfold the moments just as He unfolded the rose – Unknown Author

Seal It with a Prayer

Lord help me to concentrate on the things that are of you and separate me from the things that are not of you. In Christ Jesus Name Amen.

The Single Life – Conclusion
Single – *relating to a state of being unmarried or uninvolved in a romantic relationship*

I want you to be free from anxieties. The unmarried man is anxious about the things of the Lord, how to please the Lord. But the married man is anxious about worldly things, how to please his wife, and his interests are divided. And the unmarried or betrothed woman is anxious about the things of the Lord, how to be holy in body and spirit. But the married woman is anxious about worldly things, how to please her husband. I say this for your own benefit, not to lay any restraint upon you, but to promote good order and to secure your undivided devotion to the Lord. – 1 Corinthians 7:32-35

To the unmarried and the widows I say that it is good for them to remain single as I am. – 1 Corinthians 7:8

Let me start with I am not a therapist, marriage counselor, or a relationship counselor. But I do have life experiences in being married, living together before marriage; sex before marriage and loneliness. Let me just say this right off the top if you're not ready don't do it. I was married at age 21, wanting to be grown, trying to feel my way through life. Leaving my mother house was not a good idea. My husband and I left Baltimore to live in his hometown (I won't mention the hometown) when I get there first wrong thing was living with his parents, and then he wanted me to stay home on the weekends while he went out and had a good time, I was not allowed to go, then he wanted me to look for a job in a strange town I knew nothing about and was not given time to get to know my surroundings. To top it off I found out that my engagement and wedding rings was his former fiancée's rings. Now if I wanted to stay at someone's home I could have stayed with my mother. He wasn't an abusive person but, he was not a ready person as far as being married neither was I. So I returned to Baltimore without my husband, stay married about six-months to a year and then got an annulment.

I met my daughter's father, around age twenty-five on and off we lived together for ten years, he was my best friend, we had good times, fights and disagreements, through it all we always agreed that we loved each other very much. We decided to get married after being together almost eleven year, sadly before we could plan for the wedding he had a massive heart attack, the Lord took him home, I was devastated. After his death, at age thirty-eight, I give my life to Christ and became a servant of God. I grieved for a very long time and it seemed like I would find myself looking for my love and best friend around every corner.

I was still a babe in Christ, so a lot of my old habits was still there, I allowed my son's father to move in with me, now that I look back it was lust not love. Out of that short relationship I conceived a son, my son's father has never been a part of his life since conception, it's not that he didn't have the opportunity, he just choose not to be in his life.

After my son birth at age 41, my healing process began, I needed to heal from being married and losing someone that I loved very much. I decided that it was time to pursue a bonding relationship with Jesus. I begin to read the Bible. While reading the Bible it felt like I was searching for my life, ladies, the things I had lost, the hurt that I felt, the why's and the why not's, this was my healing period for next five years. There has been two other guys since then, mistakes made, lessons learned. Through it all the one thing I could count on was the word of God. At age fifty-nine I continue to read, study, fellowship, and build a relationship with God. I learn a lot about me, it's not who you with it what you allow, how you present yourself. I learned first to find me, what I wanted in a relationship and what I was willing to settle for also I learned that when you are in a relationship, serious or not there's are always feeling involved whether you're separated, married or unmarried. That is why we should always know who we are moreover, if you're coming out of a hurtful relationship, married or unmarried we should always have a healing period for as long as it takes, it is so unfair to the next person to bear your pain, hurt, uncertainty, and mistrust from a previous relationship or marriage and then there is the number one solution pray and wait on God for the best, he knows your heart.

Name it and Claim it...

Pray this month that God will send you a man that loves God first; that have your best interest at heart Claim it, believe it and trust God for it. Stand back and watch God do it.

Author's Reflection

Respect Yourself!

May I move beyond hurt, but not look beyond the one who has caused it. Today I will honor even those who cause me pain. ~ Anon

Dating is very hard you are constantly trying to impress the person that you want to get to know. You are constantly trying to sustain from sex which is a very hard thing to do. Sex is a hard and difficult test, a relationship test, it just like preparing for a Math test you study for it, you know it, but when you sat down to take the test your mind goes blank. We meet these guys and as women we say I' going to prepare myself. I've been hurt before, but this time I'm going to take it slow and think it through, keep myself and focus on the test at hand which is sex. But just as soon as we're sure we can pass and get ready to set down to take the test "boom" our mind goes blank, and we start given into our lust, and we fail the test. The man gets what he wants, stays for a couple of days and then "roll out" in some cases, we set ourselves up. We say to ourselves how did I failed that test again. I thought I knew it. So we start studying again preparing ourselves for the next test. The Bible says be "wise as a serpent but gentle as a dove." We have to be wise to where and how far concerning our emotions, and gentle in making him desire us, not us desiring him

And when you stand praying, if you hold anything against anyone, forgive them, so that your Father in heaven may forgive you your sins. ~ Mark 11:25

Fruit of the Spirit
The Series
May - December

Love

Joy

Peace

Patience

Kindness

goodness

Faithfulness

Self-control

Gentleness

Fruit of the Spirit

God's Single Sisters Newsletter

Verses and Scriptures - May Volume 23

The Fruit of the Spirit

Fruit – product, outgrowth

Spirit – strength, courage, character, will, strength of mind

<u>Love</u>
Romans 12:18-21
Jeremiah 31:1-6
John 13:31-35

<u>With Love</u>
How I give you up, Ephraim? How can I hand over, Israel? My heart churns within me; my sympathy is stirred – Hosea 11:8

<u>Love</u>
Love sent the savior to die in my stead. Why should He love Me so? Meekly to Calvary's cross he was led. Why should He love Me so? – Harkness

Solomon Says 📖

To know wisdom, and instruction; to perceive the words of understanding; to receive the instruction of wisdom, justice, and judgment, and equity, to give subtlety to the simple to the young man knowledge and discretion – Proverbs 1:1-4

All about You....
Name five things that you love about someone
1.
2.
3.
4.
5.
In Christ Jesus Name

Women of the Bible

Hamutal mean- Kinsman of the dew
The daughter of Jeremiah of Libnah, wife of King Josiah, and Mother of King Jehoshaz also of King Zedekiah – 2 Kings 23:31, 24:18

Jermia mean- dove
The eldest of Job's three daughters born after the time of trail – Job 42:14

Love
Anyone who does not love does not know God, because God is love. – 1 John 4:8

*L*earning – the word of God is knowledgeable and very powerful

*O*rganize – your time to read and mediate on the word of God

*V*aluable – the words of God value is greater than silver and gold

*E*verlasting – Is His Love.......

Seal It with a Prayer

Lord I thank you for your love. I thank you because your love is so perfect you died for us. No one on this earth or under the earth has that kind of love. In Christ Jesus Name Amen.

The Fruit of The Spirit - Love
Love - *a person or thing that one loves, an intense feeling of deep affection.*

Love is patient and kind; love does not envy or boast; it is not arrogant or rude. It does not insist on its own way; it is not irritable or resentful; it does not rejoice at wrongdoing, but rejoices with the truth. Love bears all things, believes all things, hopes all things, and endures all things. Love never ends. As for prophecies, they will pass away; as for tongues, they will cease; as for knowledge, it will pass away. – Corinthians 1:13:40-8

Emotional Love
A glad heart makes a cheerful face, but by sorrow of heart the spirit is crushed. – Proverbs 15:13

We're always telling our children to do the best they can, but when we see C's on their report card instead, of B's and A's the first thing we say is "you could have done better". Instead, we should rejoice with our child or children asking them "how can I help you to be the best you can be?"

Physical Love
For while bodily training is of some value, godliness is of value in every way, as it holds promise for the present life and also for the life to come. 1 Timothy 4:8

We can exercise to get that fit body, which is a good thing, but as we get older, we have to be real, those muscles tend to unshaped, sag and become droopy but godliness will never change, the things that God has promise us will never unshaped it will always reshape our lives.

Mental Love

Live in harmony with one another. Do not be haughty, but associate with the lowly. Never be wise in your own sight. – Romans 12:16

God has created us in his image. Even though we all are different, we should not think of ourselves better than the next person.

Spiritual Love

All Scripture is breathed out by God and profitable for teaching, for reproof, for correcting and training in righteousness, so that the servant of God may be thoroughly, equipped for every good work. – 1 Tim. 3:16-17

Name it and Claim it...

Pray this month that God will send you a man that loves God first. Claim it, believe it and trust God for it. Stand back and watch God do it.

Author's Reflection

The Greatest Love Ever....

May the power of your love, O Lord, fiery and sweet as honey, Wean my heart from all that is under heaven, so that I may die of your love, you who were so good as to die for my love. – St. Francis of Assisi

Think on these things...

- *God love us so much his desire was to create us and create the things to make us comfortable.*

- *God's love is so great he understands our sins*

- *God's love for us was so great when Jesus die on the cross and sat on the right side of God, he sends us a comforter which is the Holy Spirit.*

- *God loves us he shows his love through the Old Testament and New Testaments by way of the Holy Bible.*

- *God love us so much until he hid his face from Jesus while Jesus was taken all our sins upon himself on the cross.*

📖 God love us so much that his love for us is never ending from now until eternity it will never die.

In The Name Of Jesus Amen

For God so loved the world that he gave his only Son, so that everyone who believes in him may not perish but may have eternal everlasting life ~ John 3:16

God's Single Sisters
Newsletter

Verses and Scriptures - June Volume 24

The Fruit of the Spirit

Fruit – product, outgrowth

Spirit – strength, courage, character, will, strength of mind

<u>Joy</u>
Isaiah 12
1 Peter 1:19, 4:12-19
Matthew 5:1-12

<u>Joyful</u>
Then let us adore and give him His right. All glory and power, all wisdom and might, all honor and blessing; and thanks never ceasing for infinite love – Wesley

Make a joyful noise unto the Lord, all ye lands – Psalms 100

<u>Joy to the World</u>
The word became flesh and dwelt among us we beheld His glory, the glory as of the only-begotten of the Father full of grace and truth. – John 1:14

Solomon Says 📖

The way of the sluggard is blocked with thorns, but the path of the upright is a highway – Proverbs 15:19

All about You....
Name five things that gives you joy
1.
2.
3.
4.
5.
In Christ Jesus Name

Women of the Bible

Anna mean—grace
This is the name of an aged widow mentioned in the Bible. She was the daughter of Phanuel. She was a prophetess, like Miriam, Deborah, and Huldah -2 Chronicle 34:22

Gomer mean - complete or vanishing
Daughter of Dibliam who (probably in vision only) became the wife of Hosea. -Hosea 1:3

Joy
My lips will shout for joy, when I sing praises to you; my soul also, which you have redeemed. -Psalms 71:23

*J*oyful – praises and music unto the Lord
*O*pen – your mind and heart to the word of God
*Y*es – to his will, his ways and his words

Seal It with a Prayer
Father so many people are so unhappy because their joy have been stolen, Lord speak in to their spirit and restore their joy. In Christ Jesus Name Amen.

The Fruit of the Spirit – Joy
Joy - a feeling of great pleasure and happiness.

In All Circumstance
God desires us to have Joy in our lives even when circumstance become like Job. Job was a prosperous farmer living in Uz. Satan was allowed by God to come in and destroy things around Job as a testing of his faithfulness. Job was tested because Satan claimed that he was a rich wealthy man. Job was tested when his friends told him to confess his sins when he was innocent. Job had a solid foundation of faith to keep the Joy in him.

In Hard Times
When times are hard we still have Joy. For his anger endure but for a moment; in his favor is life weeping may endure for a night, but joy comes in the morning – Psalm. 30:5

Suffering and trails like Paul and Silas who have received such a charge, thrust them into the inner prison, and made their feet fast in the stocks and at midnight Paul and Silas prayed, and sang praises unto God: and the prisoners heard them. – Acts 16:24:25

It's wonderful to have joy in our lives no matter what the trail may be because of...
> the glorious birth of Christ
> the precious life of Jesus

the sacrifice that Jesus made for us
the resurrection of Jesus

Keeping Your Joy
    looking at people through the eyes of Jesus with love and compassion.
    follow and trust the Lord do not lean on your own understanding
    allow God to direct your path

Be Careful Don't Lose Your Joy
Our Joy can be lost from a lack of...
    our spiritual walk
    spiritual pride and anger

Name it and Claim it...

Pray this month that God fills your life with Joy in all circumstances. Claim it, believe it, and trust God for it. Stand back and watch God do it.

Author's Reflection

This Joy I Have.....

There are joys which long to be ours. God sends ten thousand truths, which come about us like birds seeking inlet; but we are shut up to them, and so they bring us nothing, but sit and sing awhile upon the roof, and then fly away. Anon

I rejoice greatly in the Lord that at last you have renewed your concern for me. Indeed, you have been concerned but you had no opportunity to show it. I am not saying this because I am in need for I have learned to be content whatever the circumstances. I know what it is to be in need, and I know what it is to have plenty. I have the secret of being content in any and every situation, whether well-fed or hungry, whether living in plenty or in want. I can do all things through Christ who strengthens me. ~ Philippians~ 4:10-13

I will ask the Father, and he will give you another advocate, to be with you forever. This is the Spirit of truth, whom the world cannot receive, because it neither see him nor knows him ~ John 14:16-17

This World Didn't Give It To Me, This World Can't Take It Away....

God's Single Sisters Newsletter

Verses and Scriptures - July Volume 25

The Fruit of the Spirit

Fruit – product, outgrowth

Spirit – strength, courage, character, will, strength of mind

Peace
Psalm. 34:11-14
Colossians 3:15
1 Peter 3:8-12

Peace
This is the peace God brings to those who have been reconciled to God by faith in His Son Jesus – Ephesian 2:14-16

God's Peace
The Peace of God, which surpasses all understanding well guard your hearts and your minds. – Philippians 4:7

Solomon Says 📖
My mouth speaks what is true for my lips detest wickedness all the words of my mouth is just to the discerning all of them are rights they are fruitless to those who have knowledge. – Proverbs 8:7-9

All about You....
Name five things that gives you peace
1.
2.
3.
4.
5.
In Christ Jesus Name

Women of the Bible

Anammeliah mean - Anu is king
This was the name of the Oni gods. It was a female deity representing the Moon.

Hazeleponi (Hazzeldponi) mean - the shadow look in on me; the shade turns towards me.
From the tribe of Judah. Her father was Etam. Her sisters Jezereel, Ishama and Ithash –
1 Chronicles 4:3

Poem for the Month
Life is a Journey
Life is but a stopping place, a pause in what's to be, a resting place along the road, to sweet eternity, we all have different paths along the way, to learn something but never meant to stay... Our destination is a place, far greater than we know. For some journeys quicker, for some the journey's slow. And when the journey finally ends, we'll claim a great reward, and find an everlasting place, together with the Lord – Anon

Seal It with a Prayer
Lord today I ask you to keep me safe and healthy to send your Angels around me to give me peace and joy and to cover me with your blood in Christ Jesus Name Amen.

The Fruit of the Spirit – Peace
Peace - *freedom from disturbance; quiet and tranquility, freedom from or the cessation of war or violence.*

What We Gain Through Peace
Trust in the Lord forever, for the Lord, the Lord himself, is the Rock eternal. He humbles those who dwell on high, he lays the lofty city low; he levels it to the ground and casts it down to the dust. Feet trample it down— the feet of the oppressed, the footsteps of the poor. The path of the righteous is level; you, the Upright One, make the way of the righteous smooth. Yes, Lord, walking in the way of your laws, we wait for you; your name and renown are the desire of our hearts. My soul yearns for you in the night; in the morning my spirit longs for you. When your judgments come upon the earth, the people of the world learn righteousness. But when grace is shown to the wicked, they do not learn righteousness; even in a land of uprightness they go on doing evil and do not regard the majesty of the Lord. Lord, your hand is lifted high, but they do not see it. Let them see your zeal for your people and be put to shame; let the fire reserved for your enemies consume them. Lord, you establish peace for us; all that we have accomplished you have done for us. - Isaiah 26:4-12

Perfect Peace through the Spirit
    inward peace with God
    peace of conscience

peace at all times and circumstances

Tranquility through Peace – Colossians 3:15-17
    in your heart
    with psalms, hymns and spiritual songs
    with thankfulness

Truly, I tell all of you emphatically, whoever hears what I say and believes in the one who sent me has eternal life and will not be judged, but has passed from death to life. Truly, I tell all of you emphatically, the time approaches, and is now here, when the dead will hear the voice of the Son of God, and those who hear it will live. Just as the Father has life in himself, so also he has granted the Son to have life in himself, and he has given him authority to judge, because he is the Son of Man. - John 5:24-27

Peace emphatically
    trusting his words
    his promises
    his provisions

For it is he who is our peace. Through his mortality he made both groups one by tearing down the wall of hostility that divided them. He rendered the Law inoperative, along with its commandments and regulations, thus creating in himself one new humanity from the two, thereby making peace, and reconciling both groups to God in one body through the cross, on which he eliminated the hostility. He came and proclaimed peace for you who were far away and for you who were near. - Ephesians 2:14-17

Permanent Peace
    repentance prayer
    studying the word
    meditation

Name it and Claim it...
Pray this month that God gives you perfect peace in your storms and circumstances throughout your journey. Claim it, believe it, and trust God for it. Stand back and watch God do it Jesus Name. Amen

Author's Reflection

The Perfect Peace

♡ *You will keep in perfect peace those whose mind is steadfast, because they trust in you ~ Isaiah 26:3*

♡ For he himself is our peace, who has made the two groups one and has destroyed the barrier, the dividing wall of hostility – Ephesians 2:14

♡ But the wisdom that comes from heaven is first of all pure; then peace-loving, considerate, submissive, full of mercy and good fruit, impartial and sincere. Peacemakers who sow in peace reap a harvest of righteousness – James 3:18

♡ And the peace of God, which transcends all understanding, will guard your hearts and your minds in Christ Jesus – Philippians 4:7

♡ In peace I will both lie down and sleep, for you, Lord, alone make me dwell in safety and confident trust – Psalms 4:8

♡ Peace I leave with you; my peace I give you. I do not give to you as the world gives. Do not let your hearts be troubled and do not be afraid – John 14:27

God's Single Sisters
Newsletter

Verses and Scriptures – August Volume 26

The Fruit of the Spirit

Fruit – product, outgrowth

Spirit – strength, courage, character, will, strength of mind

Patience (long suffering)
Exdous 34:6
2 Peter 3:1-9
Hebrews 12:1-13

God said stay still my child, patient and endure, I will be back that's for sure. Don't worry, don't stress, just stand still and I will do the rest – G. Bess

Make hasten to help me O'Lord – Psalms. 70:1

Patience
Our wrath uncurbed will not fulfill God's perfect plan for us, we must be patient and refuse to fret, to fume to fuss – Sper

Be patient show your world what God is really like the fruit of the spirit is long suffering – Galatians 5:16-24

The Psalmist Says ♫

How good God pleasant it is when brothers live together in unity! It is like precious oil poured on the hair running down on the beard, running down on Aaron's beard, down up on the collar of his robes. It is as if the dew of Hermon were falling on Mount Zion: for there the Lord bestows his blessing, even life forever more – Psalms 133

All about You....
Name five things you can teach yourself, on how to be patient
1.
2.

3.
4.
5.
In Christ Jesus Name

Women of the Bible

Kezia (Cassia) mean - sweet-scented spice
The name of Job's second daughter born after prosperity had returned to him – Job 42:14

Meshullemeth mean - friend
The wife of Manasseh, and the mother of Amon Kings of Judah – 2 Kings 21:19

Julia mean - Jupiter's child, downy
A Christian woman at Rome to whom Paul sent his salvation supposed to be the wife of Philologus – Roman 16:15

Poem for the Month

<u>Trust the Lord</u>
Until I learned to trust the Lord, I never learned to pray; and never to fully trust, Til sorrow came my way. Until I felt my weakness His strength I never knew, nor dreamed, Til, I was stricken that He could see me through. He who drinks deepest sorrow, drinks deepest too of grace God sends the storm, so He himself, can give us resting place. His heart who seeks our deepest good, knows well when thing annoy; we would not yarn for Heaven if earth held only joy! Author Unknown

Seal It with a Prayer

Thank you, Lord for teaching us to be patient in everything we do. Give us patience whether it's picking up a pencil, chastising a child or waiting in a long line at the grocery store.
In Christ Jesus Name. Amen.

<u>The Fruit of the Spirit—Patience</u>
Patience - *the capacity to accept or tolerate delay, trouble, or suffering without getting angry or upset.*

<u>What Do We Gain By Being Patience</u>
Be still before the Lord and wait patiently for him; fret not yourself over the one who prospers in his way, over the man who carries out evil devices! Refrain from anger, and forsake wrath!

Fret not yourself; it tends only to evil. For the evildoers shall be cut off, those who wait for the Lord shall inherit the land. Psalms 37:7-9

Learning how to be tolerance
be humble in all situations
be gentle, when you speak and when you answer

Self-restraint
control your anger
control your weakness
rejoice for others that prosper

Be Patient
We put no stumbling blocks in anyone's path so that our ministry will not be discredited. Rather, as servants of God we commend ourselves in every way: in great endurance' in troubles hardships, and distress; in beating, imprisonments and riots; in hard work, sleepless nights and hunger in purity, understanding, patience and kindness.—2 Corinthians. 6:3-6

Name it and Claim it...
Pray this month that God gives you patient each time your life goes through changes. Claim it, believe it, and trust God for it. Stand back and watch God do it.

Author's Reflections

Changes

If we begin with certainties, we shall end in doubts; but if we begin with doubts, and are patient in them, we shall end in certainties ~ Francis Bacon

I have never been a fan of changes; some changes are hard for me to accept especially when the changes to me, doesn't make good sense.

I remember when my job moved to another location, it seemed like a new start, and I was okay with it but I found out others were being promoted. I felt that all the years and all the dedication, I should have vast in the rewards and reaped the benefit of a promotion. The things that was disturbing to me was the Administrative's decisions to promote and up lift certain people and set others in a corner. I felt like a piece of paper being toss in the wind.

I felt if staff had been encouraged more, than they would have known how to encourage the clients that this center served. Should Administrators' encouragement be equal, or should it be just for the staff "that they favor"? When changes come about on a job shouldn't staff that put in dedicated years be promoted to progress not to regress and reap demotion? I'm confused how does this work?

I had a big issue of how things were being done and how certain staff was favored. I am so glad that my God doesn't promote, or bless us according to His favorite choice of people. I was so upset and disappointed, that I allowed this feeling to consume me. One Sunday when I was having my pity party, I did not go to Church, actual I'm glad I didn't because I received a message through the radio that lifted my spirit.

I was listening to the radio that morning and a Pastor came on and the Pastor was talking about Changes. I felt he was talking directly to me! He preached on the last chapters of Deuteronomy and the beginning of Joshua I cannot recall the exact chapters or verses, but he talked about the Promise Land. He said we need to:

1. Let Go ~ If your life is going through changes let it go leave it alone! Go on through the changes.
2. Shift in Neutral ~ After the change has been made or decided, sometimes we have to shift in neutral; we have to do things we don't want to do while the promise is in process.
3. Move forward to the Promise Land ~ Move forward to all the things that God promised us, for example, birthing your ministries etc.
4. Make your change by:
   a. Pursing your purpose and understanding your purpose, worship God, work for him.
   b. Proceeding to walk into your promise, what you want to do, what you desire, don't look back. Proceed forward, even if things does not go as smoothly as you would like still proceed. Remember don't look back!
   c. Process your promise. Do not fight, question, or give in to anyone, don't try to put anyone down, know your purpose.

To God Be the Glory! Many thanks to the Pastor for that wonderful and uplifting message. Ladies endure, I need you to hear this, when changes get too hard for you don't let it consume you because remember God have you at that place for a reason. Let me tell you my reason, I remember being very upset when I was told I was going to sit at the front desk as a receptionist, all my responsibilities from the old building was strip away. I went home cried and had my little pity party, I found myself not being as pleasant as usual, and I was not myself, then one morning while getting ready for work, God spoke to me He said "I put you on the front line because you know my words (the word of God) and you will be able to minister to others. I put you there for a time until I see fit to remove you". It was indeed a battle on both of my jobs nevertheless, I am looking forward to the promise.

So if that change comes and you feel you can't handle it think on these things:

- Faith is the assurance of things hoped for the evidence of things not seen ~ Hebrews 11:1
- Know that I am with you and will keep you wherever you go, and I will bring you back to this land; for I will not leave you until I have done what I have promised you. ~ Genesis 28:15
- When tempted to worry about how things will turn out. Use this memory test: What was I worrying about this time last year! In Christ Jesus Name. Amen.

God's Single Sisters Newsletter

The Fruit of the Spirit

Fruit – product, outgrowth

Spirit – strength, courage, character, will, strength of mind

Kindness (Hospitality)
Luke 14:12-14
Romans 12:13

Kindness
Father, help me live today with thoughtfulness in what I say, confronting wrong with truth and fact, expressing gentleness and tact – Hess

Proverbs Says 📖

A gentle answer turns away wrath, but a harsh word stirs up anger – Proverbs 15:1

All about You....
Name five things that makes you hospitable

1.

2.

3.

4.

5.
In Christ Jesus Name

Women of the Bible

Sapphira mean- beautiful
The wife of Ananias. She was a partner in his guilt and also in his punishment –
Acts 5:1-11

Drusilla mean - fruitful or dewy-eyed
The third and youngest daughter of Herod Agrippa I - Acts 12:1-4, 20-23

Herodias mean - Feminine form of Herod
The daughter of Aristobulus and Bernice - Matthew 14:3-11; Mark 6:17-28; Luke 3:19

Joanna mean - whom Jehovah has graciously given
The wife of Chuza, the steward of Herod Antipas, Tetrarach of Galilee – Luke 8:3.
She was one of the women who ministered to our Lord, and to whom he appeared after his resurrection – Luke 8:3, 24, 10

Poem for the Month
Kindness is not blindness. Kindness is oneness-awareness. Blindness is failure: Failure within, failure without. The awakened mind may show kindness to those who not only do not deserve it but also misuse it-alas! My Lord tells me, that my mind's cleverness-smile will never be a match for my heart's kindness-smile you can show your sweetest kindness even to those who are vehemently standing in your way. But under no circumstances must you surrender to their way. Follow not your blindness-mind; follow only your kindness-heart! - Sri Chinmoy

Seal It with a Prayer
Lord teach me to be kind to everyone that I meet, even when I think that they do not deserve it, in Christ Jesus name Amen

The Fruit of the Spirit— Kindness (Hospitality)
Kindness (Hospitality) - the quality of being friendly, generous, and considerate

What Do We Gain By Being Kind
Note then the kindness and the severity of God: severity toward those who have fallen, but God's kindness to you, provided you continue in his kindness. Otherwise, you too will be cut off. And even they, if they do not continue in their unbelief, will be grafted in, for God has the power to graft them in again. For if you were cut from what is by nature a wild olive tree, and grafted, contrary to nature, into a cultivated olive tree, how much more will these, the natural branches, be grafted back into their own olive tree. – Romans 11:22-24

Kindness is:
    the way we feel and act toward others
    making people feel comfortable
    helping each other
Kindness is not:
    being selfish

being prideful and always boasting
bad attitudes
improper uses of language

Remembering the:
homeless people
institutionalized people
people in prison
people who are in nursing homes
and most importantly our juvenile
youth

Be careful to be **<u>Kind</u>** to people, without God's favor, grace and mercy, we're only a step away from being in their positions

Name it and Claim it...
Pray this month that God will teach you how to be more hospitable toward strangers, families and children. Claim it, believe it and trust God for it. Stand back and watch God do it.

Author's Reflections

<u>*Hey! Was That An Angel?*</u>

You cannot do a kindness too soon, for you never know how soon it will be too late – Waldo Emesson

Be Kind to someone and someone will be kind to you. This is what I experience: I'll never forget one day when I was walking to the store this lady approach me, she said she was hungry. I ask her to come follow me to my house. When, we arrived to the house I invited her in. I asked if she was okay, she said that she was homeless and had slept on the bus stop bench all night. I ask her if she was a praying woman, and she said yes. We begin to pray, after prayer I fixed her some sandwiches and gave her a glass of juice. While eating she, began to ministered to my daughter (at that time my daughter was 11), she told her to always listen to your mother. She shared with my daughter if she had listened to her mother she would not have been traveling down this road. I praise God for her because she encouraged my daughter right at the time when she needed it. After that day I saw the lady walking down the street after that I never saw the lady again. Could she have been an Angel?

On a cool spring day when I was done grocery shopping, I headed to the checkout counter to pay for my groceries. My groceries total was a little more than I anticipated, as I was sorting out what foods to return, the lady behind me offered to pay the rest of the money left on my grocery bill. Could she have been an Angel?

On a chilly fall day when I went marketing with the intentions of buying a couple of things instead, I had about eight grocery bags of food and since I did not drive I had no idea how I was going to get these groceries home. I didn't have

any money to catch a hack or a cab the only transportation I could afford was the transit bus. With all those bag, it would have been too much and then I had two blocks to walk before reaching the apartment building where I lived. But I had to get home, so I decided to go ahead and catch the bus. While standing at the bus stop a lady drove up and said to me "I saw you at the market with those bags that's too much for you to carry, would you like a ride?" I said "yes, but I do not have any money." She said "don't worry about it, come on get in". Could she have been an Angel?

On a cold winter's night when I was at the supermarket a lady asked me could I spare some money to help feed her children? I gave her twenty dollars. Could she have been an Angel?

Do not neglect to show hospitality to strangers, for by doing that some have entertained Angels without knowing it – Hebrews 13:2

God's Single Sisters Newsletter

The Fruit of the Spirit

Fruit – product, outgrowth

Spirit – strength, courage, character, will, strength of mind

Goodness
Exodus 33:19, 34:6
Psalms 9:17, 23:6, 31:19, 65:11
Zechariah 33:5

The word which they heard did not profit them, not being mixed with faith. - Hebrews 4:2

God's Goodness
Drink deep of God's goodness, His faithfulness too, leave no room for doubling and fear; His word of life pure and true. Refreshing and cooling and clear – Hess

The Psalmist Says ♫

As the deer pants for streams of water so my soul pants for you, O' God. My soul thirst for God, for the living God? – Psalms 42:1-2

All about You....
Name five things that shines through your goodness towards people

1.

2.

3.

4.

5.
In Christ Jesus Name

Women of the Bible

Phebe/Phoebe mean - pure or radiant as the moon
A notable woman in the church of Cenchreae, she was trusted by Paul to deliver his letter to the Romans. – Romans 16:1-2

Lois mean - more desirable or better
The Grandmother of Timothy. She is commended by Paul for her faith. - 2 Timothy 1:5

Eunice mean - Good victory, joyous victory, she conquers
Mother of Timothy also commend for her faith. - 2 Timothy 1:5

Poem for the Month

<u>He is Always There</u>

We can't foresee the turning of the tide when problems beset us and tears are cried. Sometimes life deals from the bottom of the deck filling us with worry and leave us a wreck. The enemy seeks to devour and destroy using deceptions to eliminate our joy. While, walking through the valley our heads hang low. The mountain top streams so high, our footsteps slow. How many times have we traveled this road to battle the frustrations of troubles bestowed? Yet when we come to our drunkest hour God demonstrates His infinite, power. It does motto how bad things might seem, he always comes through our faith to redeem. God will not fail us in our times of rain. He'll never forsake us by our side he will remain. See if we lend ourselves at a total loss or when the valley seems too wide to cross just remember you're in his love and care look over your shoulder, and he's always there. – Anon

Seal It with a Prayer

Jesus I thank you for your Grace, Mercy, Love, Goodness and Favors. God I thank you for Jesus and Jesus I thank you for your Holy Spirit. In Christ Jesus Name. Amen.

<u>The Fruit of the Spirit— Goodness</u>

Goodness - *the quality of being good, in particular*

<u>Seeing the Goodness of God</u>

And we know that for those who love God all things work together for good, for those who are called according to his purpose. For those whom he foreknew he also predestined to be conformed to the image of his Son, in order that he might be the firstborn among many brothers. And those whom he predestined him also called, and those whom he called he also justified, and those whom he justified he also glorified. – Romans 8:28-30

Things that work for the Good: trusting God in all situations, loving him and allowing God to work it out, believing in his word in his promises, knowing your purpose, your ministry

Goodness is:
   being generous
   being kind
   having good will
   being merciful

I'm still confidence in this I will see the goodness of the Lord in the land of the living. Wait for the Lord; be strong and take heart and wait for the Lord. – Psalm 27:13-14

Name it and Claim it...

Pray this month that God show you how to see the goodness in people. Even when, people that are awful seems to shine. Claim it, believe it, trust God for it and Stand back and watch God do it....

Author's Reflection

I Better Recognize!

I appreciate the goodness of my family and our relationship. No matter what we say as siblings, we always had each other backs. I would like to pause today to thank and recognize my family, my mother, sisters, brothers, children and grandchildren.

Children – To my daughter Shaniece, I thank you for your strength. For being that brave little girl, who hung in there when mommy was weak. For putting your arms around me when I was sad and telling me somehow it was going to be alright. You always knew when I was upset even when I tried to hide it. To my son Jeremiah I thank you for your wisdom, your knowledge and curiosity and love for God's planets and living creatures. You seem to see the beauty in God's world that no one else seems to see. To Neveah my granddaughter, from an infant I saw God's protection around you. Thank you for being you, you have such a beautiful spirit, your boldness and sense of humor is a blessing. To little Devin when you were born I saw the gentleness in your spirit. I saw the strength that you inherit from your mother; I saw the happiness that you brought to everyone. Thank you, Lord for this baby. Thank you, Lord for my children and grandchildren.

To my mother I thank you for your kindness, your spirit of gentleness and your love without these things I would not be who I am.

To my brother Edgar I thank you for your spirit and knowledge of Math.

To my brother Roland I thank you for your spirit of giving.

To my sister Stephanie I thank you for your gift of cooking, decorating and your spirit of hospitality.

To my sister Cherrice I thank you for the gift of negotiation and your spirit of encouragement

Grand children is the crown of the aged; and the glory of children is their parents – Proverbs 12:6

God's Single Sisters
Newsletter

Verses and Scriptures ~November Volume 29

The Fruit of the Spirit

Fruit – product, outgrowth

Spirit – strength, courage, character, will, strength of mind

<u>Faithfulness</u>
Psalms 78, 111
Lamentation 3:22-32
Galatians 5:16-26

There can be time when our minds are in doubt, times when our faith is in doubt, but we can believe him. We know that he cares—Our God is real as the Bible declares—Fitzbugh

Thomas answered and said to Him "My Lord and My God!" - Luke 18:27

<u>Walking</u>
He walks with me, and He talks with me, and He tells me I am His own, and the joy we share as we tarry there none other has ever known. Enoch walked with God; and he was not, for God took him—Genesis 5:24

The Psalmist Says ♫

Trusting Him at all times O' people; pour out your hearts to him, for God is our refuge. — Psalm 62:8

All about You....
Name five things that you're committed to in your walk of faith.
1.
2.
3.
4.
5.
In Christ Jesus Name

Women of the Bible

Martha mean – bitterness
The sister of Lazarus and Mary, and probably the eldest of the family, who all resided at Bethany - Luke 10:38, 40, 41; John 11:1-39

Nagge mean - illuminating
One of the ancestors of Christ in the maternal line—Luke 3:25

Nymphas mean - nymph
Saluted by Paul in his Epistle to the Colossians as a member of the church of Lavdicia—Colossians 4:15. It was not known if this was a man or woman.

A Piece of History
Okay yawl, I have never been a person who like politics. I never had any interest in listening to the news about potential candidates. But this particular Presidential campaign, captured my interest. I watched the debates and listened to the news. In this campaign I saw Martin Luther King I had A Dream speech come alive again, I heard the cries of the poor and needy. I saw babies that God raised up to lead His people out of the land of poverty. I saw History being made on this day (November 4, 2008) the day I turned 50. God Bless Obama and his family.

Thanksgiving
Give thanks always and for everything to God the Father in the name of our Lord Jesus Christ - Ephesians 5:20

*T*hanksgiving – express your gratitude especially to God

*H*eart – give from your heart

*A*ppreciate – what God has given you, so you can understand the needs of others

*N*eighbor – love your neighbors

*K*indness – be kind to those who are not as blessed, to have the things you have

*S*hare – your time, volunteer

Seal It with a Prayer

Lord I am so thankful today that you allowed me to see a half of a century. You allow me to see my daughter become an adult with her own children, to see the birth of both of my grandchildren, to hug, kiss and love my son. You allowed me to love and receive all the things that you have blessed me within this year and the coming years. I love you Lord and I thank you. In Christ Jesus Name. Amen.

The Fruit of the Spirit— Faithfulness
Faithfulness - *the quality of being faithful; fidelity.*

The Test

"Faith is the substance of things hoped for, the evidence of things not seen." - Hebrews 11:1

To the church in Smyrna write: These are the words him who is the first and the last, who died and came to life again. I know your poverty—yet you are rich! I know the slander of those who say they are Jews and are not but are a synagogue of Satan. Do not be afraid of what you are about to suffer. I tell you the devil will put some of you in prison to test you, and you will suffer persecution for ten days. Be faithful, even to the point of death, and I will give you the crown of life. He who has an ear, let him hear what the spirit says to the churches. He who overcomes will not be hurt at all by the second death – Revalation 2:8-11

Faith is:
    using your heart your soul and mind in trusting God
    positive thinking
    believing he died on the cross

Faith is not:
    falseness, doubt in your mind, heart and soul
    worrying, stressing
    disbelief in God words

One who is faithful in a very little is also faithful in much, and one who is dishonest in a very little is also dishonest in much. If then you have not been faithful in the unrighteous wealth, who will entrust to you the true riches? And if you have not been faithful in that which is another's, who will give you that which is your own? – Luke 16:10-12

Name it and Claim it...

Pray this month that God gives you strength in your walk of faith. Claim it, believe it, and trust God. Stand back and watch God do it.

Author's Reflection

<u>*Walk By Faith Not By Sight.....*</u>

Feed your faith and doubt will starve; use your faith and you will never lose it - Anon

The scripture walk by faith and not by sight is a hard thing to do, but it is also very necessary. When storms come (and the storms do come very often), I would always freeze up. What I mean by freezing is I would worry a lot, allow my flesh to get in the way, thoughts in my mind would go in different directions, and I became very emotional. But God strengthen each storm I went through I became stronger and laid back. God has taught me how to walk by faith and not by sight. It was there all the time all I had to do was trust God. I learn to speak faith through the scriptures, I learn how to seek faith by seeing God face in every circumstance, I learn how to pray those storms away, I learn how to stand on faith and I learn that God had it all in control

Jesus answered them, "Have faith in God. Truly I tell you if you say to this mountain be taken up and thrown into the sea, and if you do not doubt in your heart, but believe that what you say will come to pass, it will be done for you." - Mark 11:22-23

God's Single Sisters
Newsletter

Verses and Scriptures ~ December Volume 30

The Fruit of the Spirit

Fruit – product, outgrowth

Spirit – strength, courage, character, will, strength of mind

Gentleness
Titus 3:2
James 3:17
1 Peter

Control Yourself
A man of knowledge uses words with restraint, a man understanding is even-tempered. — Proverbs 17:27

Gentle
Lord, grant me a loving heart, a will to give a whispered prayer upon my lips to show I really care - Brandt

The Psalmist Says 🎵

Help, Lord for the godly are no more; the faithful have vanished from among men every one lies to his neighbors their flattering lips speak with deception. – Psalms 12:1-2

All about You....
Name two people that you are gentle with and name three things that you have self-control over
1.
2.
3.
4
5.
In Christ Jesus Name

Women of the Bible

Mary mean – Wished-for child; rebellion; bitter. Famous Bearers: the Virgin

Mary – Joseph wife, Mother to Jesus, Joseph, James, Judas and Simon. There is evidence of sisters as well, but they are not mention in the bible – Matthew 2:11, Matthew 1:23, Luke 1:27, Acts 1:14, Matthew 13:55 -5:6 and Mark 6:3

Mary – wife of Cleopas – John 19:25

Mary – Lazarus & Martha's sister – John 11:20, 31:33, 12:2, 11:38, 11:19

Mary - Mother of John, Mark, sister of Bannahas – Colossians 4:10, Acts 4:37, 12:12

Mary Magdalene – One of the women who ministered to Christ their substance.-Luke 8:3.

Mary – A Christian at Rome who treated Paul with special kindness – Romans 16:6 and 2 Timothy 22-23

Poem for the Month

Enduring Faith

I've dreamed many dreams that never came true. I've seen them vanish at dawn, but I've realized enough of my dreams, thank God to make me to want to dream on. I've prayed many prayers, when no answer came though I waited patient and long, but answers have come to enough of my prayer to make me keep trusting you. I've sown many a seed that fell by the way upon, but I've held enough golden shaver in my hand to make me keep sowings on I've drained the cup of disappointments and pain and gone many days without the son, but I've sipped enough nectar from the sprees of life to make me want to live on – Author unknown

Seal It with a Prayer

Lord help me to always be gentle to others as I travel this journey, give me self-control over the things that I feel like saying when my feelings are hurting, and I am being attacked from all ends, Lord keep a guard over my mouth. In Christ Jesus Name Amen.

The Fruit of the Spirit— Gentleness/Self Control (Temperance)

Gentleness - *the quality of being kind and careful.*
Self-Control - an aspect of inhibitory control, is the ability to control one's emotions and behavior in the face of temptations and impulses. As an executive function, self-control is a cognitive process that is necessary for regulating one's behavior in order to achieve goals.
Avoid
Flee the evil desires of youth and pursue righteousness, faith, love and peace, along with those who call on the Lord out of a pure heart. Don't have anything to do with foolish and

stupid arguments, because you know they produce quarrels and the Lord's servants must not quarrel; instead he must be kind to everyone able to teach, not resentful. Those who oppose him he must gently instruct, in hope that God will grant him repentance leading them to the knowledge of truth and that they will come to their senses and escape from the trap of the devil, who has taken them captive to do his will – 2 Timothy 2:21-26

Maintain
But as for you, continue in what you have learned and have become convinced of, because you know those from whom you learned it, and how from infancy you have known the holy Scriptures which are able to make you wise for salvation through faith in Christ Jesus.—2 Timothy 3:14-15

Please Be Gentle
Putting others before ourselves:
be Christ like makes people see Jesus in you be outward towards others be quick to overlook the sins of other, do not be jealous or envious. Avoid using harsh words, be spirit filled, forgiving other with all gentleness and kindness from your heart.

Gentleness is:
> compassion
> forbearance
> meekness
> sweetness

Self-control is:
> self-discipline
> self-denial
> self-assurance

Name it and Claim it...
Pray this month that God gives you a soft voice and not a harsh loud voice. Claim it, believe it, and trust God. Stand back and watch God do it.

Arthur's Reflection

Be Oh' So Gentle

Let me consider what might happen should I let another's animosity spark gentleness in me. Could the shock of it start us both on the path of friendship? – Anon
Lord help me to be gentle with:
> *my words to others*
> *the way I handle things*

- my family and friends
- being quick to judge

Lord help me to control myself when:
- I am in public or private to be disciplined
- My body, mind, desires, emotions, will, time, possessions and appetite wants to take over.

A soft answer turns away wrath, but a harsh word stirs up anger. ~ Proverbs 15:1

Fruit of the Spirit

Love is the most precious gift of them all. Love helps us to obtain the other fruits which brings us:

- Joy which gives us laughter, with our children, with our mates; when we are happy and even when we are sad.
- Peace when we need calmness, when we need rest, when we need understanding.
- Kindness to help someone that's hurting, to be nice to someone, to give encouragement.
- Goodness to be good to someone, to uplift, to smile and compliment; to make someone's day.
- Faithfulness to walk in it, to believe, embrace and trust.
- Gentleness to hug, to embrace and console.
- Self-Control to think before we speak or act upon a situation

Final Thoughts

We are made up of thousands of others. Everyone has ever done a kind deed for us or spoken one word of encouragement for us has entered into the make-up of one character and of our thoughts, as well as our success – George Matthew Adams

If one member suffers, all suffer together with it; if one member is honored all rejoice together with it –
1 Corinthians 12:26

There is no such thing as a "self-made" woman. God Bless You All –Gloria Bess

Printed in the United States
By Bookmasters